Christian Theology and Tribal Culture

Christian Heritage Rediscovered

The Series, as the name suggests, is meant to focus on Christian Faith & Living vis-à-vis topics like Literature & Poetry, Indigenous Philosophizing, Ethical response towards Agriculture, Health & Healing, Science & Technology, Ecofeminist Theology, Sociological approach towards Human Rights, Law & Politics, Arts, History of Ideas, Ancient Civilizations, Cultural Contiguity, Religious Cosmologies & Mysticism, Footsteps of famous Theologians, World Peace & Harmony, Global Capitalism, Network Marketing, Cybertheology, Population & Demographics, Epigraphic Studies, Contextualized Education, and many others. We welcome a Mss. on any topic/s mentioned, whether they are original works, scholarly monographs, collections of conference papers, revised dissertations, or translations of historical documents. Through the Series we, the Publishers, are striving to put forward published works that may help Institutions, Academic Bodies, Researchers, Scholars and the World at large in furthering their respective knowledge and understanding on the concerned subject. We welcome your comments on our efforts and further suggestions on how we can foster the upcoming thoughtful theologically grounded books.

Christian Heritage Rediscovered - 84

Christian Theology and Tribal Culture

In Dialogue with C. S. Song

Lalboi Singsit

Christian World Imprints

First Published in 2019 by

Christian World Imprints
Christian Publishing & Books from India
C-3, Shop No. 14, Ground Floor
Wazirpur Industrial Area, **Delhi-110052**
cwidelhi2017@gmail.com
www.ChristianWorldImprints.com
Phone: +91 11 41526079

ISBN: 978-93-5148-380-9

Printed in India.

DEDICATION

To
My Beloved Mother-in-Law
Late Mrs. Ngaineng Chongloi
Whose untimely departure for her heavenly abode
Left us stunned and gravely saddened us
on 12th June 2010.

Contents

Acknowledgement

I am thankful to the North India Institute of Post Graduate Theological Studies (NIIPGTS) for enrolling me to study M. Th. in Christian Theology that enabled me to undertake the present research. My sincere gratefulness goes to my mentor Rev. Dr. A. Wati Longchar, the Dean of Senate Centre for the Extension and Pastoral Theological Research (SCEPTRE), Professor of Christian Theology and Ethics, and a thesis' guide for the students of NIIPGTS (now, Principal of Taiwan Theological Seminary, Taiwan), who patiently inspired me to articulate my thoughts on tribal theology till the completion of the present research and also his compliment in the form of FORWORD owing to book publication. I am also thankful to Rev. Dr. H. Vanlalauva, the then Dean of SATHRI for his assistance as my former guide in the initial period. My sincere thanks are also due to the library staffs of Serampore and Bishop's Colleges for their kind cooperation.

I owe my thanks to my parents for their constant financial support and prayers without them my M.Th. study would have been never be completed. My thanks are also due to my father in-law Pu Ngulkam Chongloi for his moral and financial support. I owe also my special thanks to my wife Jenny Singsit who had to bear the all hardships in my fairly long absences from home during my first year of study.

My thanks are also due to Rev. Ch. Lhunkhosei Mate for his contributions in terms of theological interactions, and Mr. Thangjakhup Hangsing, Miss Tingneilhing Chongloi, and Miss Bemnu Hangsing for taking the pains of distributing and collecting the research work' questionnaires. I owe my thanks also to Rev. Asish Kumar for all necessary technical assistance and arrangement. Also, I am solely responsible for the title contents and opinion expressed in this book. Last, but not the least, I owe my thanks to Rev. Jojan Jose for his timely direction for the book publication.

Foreword

Over the years, people have developed different cultural traditions adapting to different environment. Tribal people have developed their culture around the land and its resources, while others have developed in the context of struggle for survival. Their worldview, history, stories, spirituality, community life, symbols are bound to be different.

There is neither inferior nor superior culture. There are oppressive and liberative potentials in all cultures. As a result of many years of colonization, the dominated or tribal traditions are demonized and seen as uncivilized while western culture is held superior and civilized way of life. But one should know that it is a matter of priority. Tribal people give more priority to protection of environment because the survival future humanity depends on land and its resources. All the cultural and religious practices are geared toward protection of environment. In other words, contrary to the colonizers description of the land as 'wilderness' or `empty space', tribal's worldview is radically related to the land, mountains, rocks, the entire cosmic universe and everything therein. For them, the land is the temple (cathedral), university, hospital, sustenance, the vast hall where we congregate and celebrate, and their parent and life. It is in the land that we worship, heal the sick, educate their children, and feed the people. The loss of land and the destruction of the tribal people's environment is an affront to identities, the loss of spirituality and self-determining existence. If the land and its resources are not protected, the family, clan and village and the tribe's identity and culture too would be lost. For tribals, land is thus more than just a habitat or a political boundary; it is the basis of their social organization, economic system and cultural identification. While in the western worldview, humanity is the ontological basis of all realities, the land is the basis of all realities – human selfhood and identity in indigenous worldview. Even the understanding of God differs. In western thinking, nature is something detached or outside of God. But for tribal people, God cannot be perceived apart from creation; God is in creation. The earth is sacred because God indwells in creation. Manipulation and exploitation of environment is fully justified in western ethics. For tribal people, it is rather adaptation to environment because the earth is sacred and their mother. How can we sell and exploit our mother! Therefore, viewing western culture as superior is wrong and this colonial mind-set must be changed.

Cultures are necessary tools to mediate, express and bear the Gospel. Cultures are also the womb of incarnation. Without culture we are not only unable to understand the Gospel, but provide no ground for Gospel to exist. (Huang Poho, *From Galilee to Tainan*: 79) Asians have neglected our liberative culture in doing theology for many years. This neglect has not only made our theology stranger to our people, but also could raise prophetic voice against the unjust systems and practices. More particularly, the negligence of spiritual connection between humans and earth is a serious mistake today in doing Christian theology. The ecological crisis testifies the negligence of Christian moral teaching of interrelatedness of life. Unless we recover the spiritual connection of people with the earth's family, it is not possible to talk about liberation. It is like attempting to liberate oneself after killing one's own mother. By rediscovering and reinterpreting tribal spirituality in the light of Christian teaching, tribal theologians can contribute new ways of doing theology in our search for a theology that transforms not only human community but also the whole cosmos.

Diversity of culture is God's structure of creation. It is like a rainbow. All colours are unique and different, and together with different colours make the rainbow beautiful. In the same way, God who created all, whether minority or majority traditions are unique and beautiful, and they must be respected, protected and also nurtured. Not only western cultures, tribal cultures are also richly blessed by God. Not only majority culture, but also the smallest tribe tradition is blessed by God. The world will become richer when we celebrate together in different cultures and traditions with respect and love. Christian faith and worship will be more colourful and meaningful when we incorporate our own traditions.

However, we are not saying that all our tribal cultural practices are good. We are also not saying that we should go back to traditional customs and practices. What we are saying is we should preserve and practice our customs and culture in a transformed or changed manner in the light of the teaching of Jesus Christ. Culture is not static and interaction with gospel makes culture dynamic and become a liberating force. Gospel leads us to discern human limitation and challenge us to transform, resist, and reject oppressive elements in our culture for the sake of protecting life.

C.S. Song is one of the most creative theologians in Asia. Dialoguing with Song's theology of culture and his story telling theological method, Lalboi Singsit has attempted to rediscover some of the liberative tradition of tribal culture, especially Kuki culture in interpreting Christian faith in tribal context. I am sure this work will provoke new ideas in our search for a relevant theology in tribal context.

Rev. Dr. Wati Longchar
Taiwan
15 May, 2019

Glossary

Pathen	:	God or the Holy Father
Haosa	:	Village chief
Indoi	:	A symbolical bundle of articles representing the presence of the transcendental God, hung in each and every Kuki house
Becha	:	A family relative who acts as the spokesman of a family
Tucha	:	Family stewards, usually who procure a wife from a particular family acts as steward in that family to which one procures a wife
Sunggao	:	A family relative, all the kinsmen of one's mothers
Khankho	:	The Kuki traditional way of life
Nulam	:	A family relative by virtue of taking a wife from the same family
Lom	:	Corporate labour corps
Long-man	:	A customary practice in which the maternal uncle claim a mithun as a dead price on the death of his nephew and their mother
Kut	:	Autumn or Harvest Festival of the Kukis
U-pa	:	Genealogical head of a clan or tribe
Nao-pa	:	Genealogically younger or one's brother

Som	:	Traditional Boys dormitory
Zawlbuk	:	Village dormitory for the Mizos
Lom	:	Kuki youth social organization, 'team work' or 'corporate work
Tomngaina/ Tlawmngaihna	:	It is the life principle that binds the village community together
Sobaliba	:	Ao Naga term of moral principle self-sacrifice, total self-denial, preservation, cooperation, honesty, truthfulness, industrious etc
Bulpipa	:	Chief of genealogical Kuki tribe

Introduction

Various reflections on Choan-Seng Song's[1] theology of cultures have been seen in *Asian journals* and articles at present. But it is rare or not at all seen such as A Study on C.S. Song's Theology of Cultures from Indian Perspective or particularly from the Kuki tribal perspective. Therefore, this book, *Christian Theology and Tribal Culture: In dialogue with C. S. Song* is first of its kind. Well, many may have been puzzled, confused and shocked those spellbound by time-honoured theological concepts and norms of Western theology as to whether this could be part of Christian theology? If not, distressed in a way culture has been incorporated into Christian theology assuming that Christian theology has to do only with metaphysics, lofty ideals, spiritual and divine things such as redemption from sin (salvation), church and consummation (Kingdom of God, heaven and hell) and thus, nothing to do with one's culture.

So, in the light of these confusions and misapprehensions, some clarifications are needed. Western Christian theologies are based on anthropocentric tradition/worldview that is accompanied by dualism developed under the influence of Hellenistic philosophy. Therefore, the anthropocentric view of Christian faith becomes a hermeneutic principle for the Christian interpretation of Scripture and Christian traditions. Lynn Townsend White Jr., a professor of medieval history

[1] Choan-Seng Song, hereafter the author will use as Song.

at Princeton, Stanford and UCLA has argued, "Traditional Judeo-Christian theology is fundamentally exploitative of the natural world. The mentality of the Industrial Revolution that the earth was a resource for human consumption, was much older than the actuality of machinery, and has its roots in medieval Christianity and attitudes towards nature."[2] Heup Young Kim goes on further that the anthropocosmic vision should be adopted as the foundation of ecotheology as he visualizes the unity of Heaven, Earth and Humanity in the worldview of East Asian triadic.[3] This is to indicate that our Christian theology developed within Judeo-Greco-Roman worlds has discarded the other facets of Christian theology namely, creation and culture while so being engrossed to Christological debates, especially of the divinity of Jesus over the humanity of Jesus, in which Gnosticism, Docetism and few others hold no exception that fell prey to overemphasis of spiritual mysticism, and in the course of Christian history, Christian theology turns out to be exclusive in its approach and outlooks. So, against the backdrop of this theological framework, efforts for theological exploration and a critique from Asian perspective have been undertaken so as to make Christian theology relevant, inclusive and holistic.

Charles H. Kraft identifies two things in cultural forms, conceptualizations of material items and conceptualizations of non-material items. He observes that most are conceptualizations of non-material items represented by marriage customs, family structure, words, grammatical cultural forms, singing, dancing, speaking etc.[4] Hence, all through our study of culture, it will be mostly seen from a non-material perspective. As a study is undertaken on C.S. Song's theology of cultures, the overview of Song's theological concerns over the Asian people will be appraised indigenously.

---

[2] Huang Po Ho, *Embracing the Household of God: A Paradigm Shift from Anthropocentric Tradition to Creation Responsibility in Doing Theology*, (Kolkata: PTCA, 2014), 20.

[3] Heup Young Kim, "Life Ecology, and Theo-Tao: Towards a Theology of Theanthropocosmic," in *JTCA: The Journal of Theologies and Cultures in Asia; Green Theology; An Asian Ecumenical Response to Eco-Justice*, 11(2012): 127.

[4] Charles H. Kraft, *Christianity in Culture: A Study in Dynamic Biblical Theologizing in Cross-Cultural Perspective* (New York: Maryknoll, 1981), 64.

Song is considered as one of the most creative theological writers today. His publications of books are mostly reflections on the history of Asian pains and sufferings under different imperial and colonial dominations. He is against the imposition of gospel in the westernized and modernized forms. Especially, in his theological transposition and theology of incarnation, Song attempts to totally transpose the gospel from Jesus of Nazareth of Israel to Asian lands without going through Christianity of West. His main attempt is to understand gospel from one's indigenous cultural context. By this, he advocates story theology as a medium to penetrate the hearts of the people irrespective of religion, race and nation. He finds story theology as the most suitable means. Some of his major publications include, *Christian Mission in Reconstruct—An Asian Analysis*, CLS, Madras, 1975. *Third Eye Theology*, Lutterworth, London, 1979. *The Compassionate God*, Orbis, 1982. *Theology from the Womb of Asia*. SCM, London, 1986. *Tears of Lady Meng*. WCC, 1981. *Tell Us Our Names: Story Theology from an Asian Perspective*. Orbis, New York, 1984. Besides these publications, he has also written many articles for periodicals such as *South East Asia Journal of Theology* and *International Review of Mission; JTCA: The Journal of Theologies and Cultures in Asia* and continues to write Asian from the Asian perspective.

Song takes the Asian people as his priority. He does not begin with the study of God (Doctrine of God) but with the study of humanity, the people and the world. Its raw material is not simple scriptures or traditions but the whole world with its theological structures, art, poetry and politics. He makes critical use of Asian resources to 'incarnate God's message' for Asians at large. He invites Christians to go beyond the particularities of their western cultures, to the cultures of other people. Song's central concerns in his theology are: a) Creation and universal message of God to all people b) An attempt to formulate an Asian incarnational theology c) An Asian theology of Politics d) Contextualization of theology in Asian terms. Song's understanding of Christ's incarnation enables him greatly in his theology of contextualization. In Christ's incarnation, God takes history, the people and the entire living realities seriously.[5] Therefore, Song's interest is to discover and make creative use of various obvious and hidden resources, such as history, religion, culture, traditions and folklores of the Asian people. He also challenges others to do similar contextual theology in one's own context.

In light of Song's theology of cultures, a critical study will be made on the religio-cultural context of the Kuki people. The coming of Christianity with its western culture and colonial power is without exception that has caused tremendous cultural dislocation and identity crisis, and further led to mushrooming of multiple denominations. Therefore, although the modern education and other developments of the West that came along with Christianity has been praiseworthy and a blessing in many ways for the tribals of the Northeast India, particularly the Kuki people, yet the impact of Western Christianity is also not without flaws. Such being the case, one cannot be uncritical of the consequences wrought by the western Christianity. Indisputably, the Kuki cultural history and life has become distorted with the influence of the outside. The assimilating process has enormous impact on their socio-cultural life including the patterns of thinking and ways of understanding. These cultural changes have been leading to cultural disorientation in the practices and thus, resulting to disintegration of many indigenous cultures of the people. Not only that, even the institutionalized and dogmatized Christian faith with its extreme eschatological propensities that needs to be liberated, is another aspect of worth appraising. Therefore, an attempt is made to interpret the gospel in the cultural thought forms of the people.

Although, it is not an attempt to unify all the Christians denominations of the Kuki people, which is indeed a far-cry, too, yet one cannot ignore a popular phrase, 'the unity in diversity' in want of Christianity to be a witnessing community at a larger and broader influence in the world. Needless to say, owing to the undivided community of the Kuki people, one would be apparently recalled to the event before the British colonial era—one such instance can be indicated how instantly united they were religiously, socio-

[5] S. Batumalai, *An Introduction to Asian Theology* (New Delhi: ISPCK, 1991), 63.

politically and culturally before Christianity took over their primal religious faith and culture. A glimpse of their unity can be seen in their withstanding the onslaught of the British colonial power during 1917-1919 AD, commonly known as the Kuki Rebellion or the Kuki Rising[6] that lasted about three years. There could be other several factors as to what actually made them united to that extent—three foci are inherently implicit such as religio-cultural and political urges. Sadly, the unity among the Kukis especially under the Kuki *Haosa* or chieftain system of administration that embodies the core of Kuki polity, custom and tradition has been largely disordered. The Kuki villages that were held together by social, cultural, economic, religious and political bonds were largely turned down by the British colonial power and subsequently, to their drawback, fuel was added by their new found faith. In this regards, M. Thongkhosei Haokip has rightly observed:

> The coming of Christian gospel to the far-flung and the remotest part of the world of the Kukis was a cause to be praised and celebrated and for which God is to be praised. Christianity which came as a dynamic force that spread over all the regions with the result that about 95% became followers of Christ within a span of a half century's record time. But the Christianity that the Kukis were exposed to was a divided Christianity, divided in doctrines, beliefs and practices. This was owing to the missionaries who came belonged to different denominational churches and countries. Initially it was American Baptist Mission who went to the north and the Independent Pioneer Mission started by Watkin Roberts who went to the south, other denominations followed. Today, almost all of the world's denominations are present among them.[7]

[6] Hemkhochon Chongloi, "Khankhology A Study of the Socio-Political, Religio-Cultural Norms of the Kuki People," in *An Emerging Tribal Theology from the Kuki Perspective,* edited by L. Seilen (Manipur: Trulock Theological Seminary, 2011), 91.

[7] M. Thongkhosei Haokip, *Ecumenism Among the Kukis of North East India with Special Reference to Kuki Christian Leaders Fellowship (KCLF) and Kuki Worship*

What draws our attention to most of us is a 'divided Christianity,' that exists in the forms of multiple denominations. One would perhaps observe the superfluous of an attempt towards uniformity in religious enterprises with an idea that religious conviction is personal matter hence, nothing to do with uniformity. It is true that everyone believes in 'unity in diversity' that expresses a concept about 'unity without uniformity and diversity without fragmentation.' There is nothing wrong in it. However, owing to the call and Christian witness of the gospel by a community, the authenticity of a divided Christian community church is inevitably questionable that is partly touched in this research. Kosuke Koyama in his book, *Water Buffalo Theology* aptly encapsulates how Christian mission should look like in a religiously plural world in terms of "the crucified mind" and "the crusading mind." For him "the crucified mind" is contrary to "the crusading mind." A crusading mind is a mind that is trying to subdue and take control of others – to win is to subdue and to control[8] without considering the authenticity of other religion and cultures. On the other hand, the "crucified mind" that is based on Paul's attitude, "I know nothing but "Christ crucified" (1 Cor. 2:2), Koyama calls this the 'crucified-mind,' or a crucified theology. It is an attitude of humility, eager to learn from others as well. It is a handle-less theology that does not boast in its superiority, comprehensiveness, resourcefulness, efficiency, and convenience. A handle-less theology is, therefore, a non-grabbing theology. It does not grab God or people for self-aggrandizement.[9] Similar line of thoughts has been vigorously specified by S.J. Samartha in his book, *One Christ—Many Religions* in terms of Helicopter Christology vs. Bullock-cart Christology:

> A helicopter Christology, in its attempts to land on the religious plural terrain of Asia, makes such a lot of missiological noise and kicks up so much of theological

---

Service (KWS) (Secunderabad: AICS), 59.

[8] https://lanyongxing.blogspot.com/2011/12/kosuke-koyamas-water-buffalo-theology.html (09/04/2019)

[9] https://www.goodreads.com/book/show/1757396.No_Handle_On_The_Cross, (09/04/19)

> dust that people around are prevented from hearing the voice and seeing the vision of the descending divinity. A bullock-cart Christology, on the other hand, has its wheels always touching the unpaved roads of Asia, for without the continual friction with the ground, the cart cannot move forward at all. Moreover, a bullock-cart Christology has the advantage of having its bullocks move on with a steady pace even when the driver sometimes falls asleep.[10]

True to these statements, most Christian missionaries came with the crusading mind, a mind determining to capture, take over the people and their cultures without considering what others have. What is more apparently unfortunate is their inability to appreciate and perceive the good cultures of others that are as good as theirs. Samartha has aptly observed about the mode of presenting the gospel to Asian context. Although, his argument is on the basis of 'Christology from above' and 'Christology from below,' yet it has immense relevance owing to the inability to understand the gospel by different groups of communities. As a matter of fact, the gospel presented to us does not make much sense to us as Asians; the gospel presented to the natives does not or hardly touch the ground reality, i.e., people's religious-cultural ethos or worldviews.

The whole gamut of the Kuki society revolves around *khankho*—the norm by which a person abides or being obligated to what is due to one at a given moment. The same is found in the words of Jesus Christ's ethical teaching when he says, "So when you are offering your gifts at the altar, if you remember that your brother or sister has something against you, leave your gifts there before the altar and go; first be reconciled to your brother or sister, and then come and offer your gift" (Matt. 5:23-24). This merely underlies priority of social relations (i.e. the practice of *khankho*) over the vertical relation (spiritual aspect), which means unless one fulfils what is due in terms of his/her social obligation, any spiritual act performed may turn to be sheer hypocrisy.

---

[10] S.J. Samartha, *One Christ—Many Religions: Toward a Revised Christology*, (Bangalore: SATHRI 2000), 132.

The tribals of the North Eastern parts in its pristine state were corporate, communitarian, cultured, monitored by shared ideas and belief systems. It is quite contrary to the concept of postmodernism or existential interpretation of life, salvation etc. that is based on 'here and now decision,' personal, individualism, capitalism, consumerist cultures alike. Such being the case, simply cooperating with the present trend of a cultureless Christianity would further lead us to cultural up-rootedness. Sociologically, a people without culture are nobody—there identity is nowhere. A further critique can be made here; ironically, the Kukis are united by their cultural grids but divided by their distinctive Christian denominations. The relation between gospel and culture is sharply distinguished. People are so tied with their own Christian denomination or with their new found faith, one could easily observe a paradox here whether the people are advancing in the saving knowledge of Jesus Christ or in their idiosyncratic Christian denomination! Ironically, most could die for the sake of their religious organizations rather than dying for the sake of gospel. A closer look at the existing and competing churches, one could come to the sense of churches being too carnal, hypocritical and privatized. Hence, at times one can see churches growing like any other private institutions, companies and social organizations rather than standing as the true apostolic church—the only one church under the headship of one Christ. The dichotomy of gospel and culture still exist under the grip of westernised Christianity that needs to be overcome through cultural theology.

A realization took place with the efforts of the Indian and tribal theologians amid the 20th century that started to re-locate, re-assert and reclaim the cultural values of the tribals. This was aptly recognized by Keshap Chandra Sen in early part of the 19th century that states "...West has reduced Christianity to a series of lifeless dogmas and antiquated symbols, while the East realises that what is needed is a living encounter with the living Christ whose very humanity is guaranteed, as it were, his Asian-ness."[11] For M.M. Thomas, the only valid and living theology is one which is hammered out in dialogue

[11] R.H.S. Boyd, *An Introduction to Indian Christian Theology* (Delhi: ISPCK, 2006), 30.

with these different viewpoints, a theology arising from what he calls a 'dialogical situation. He necessitates that theology must do its works not in isolation from but in dialogue with the new Hindu philosophy and theology.[12] Tribals or any other race or community are not without their own philosophy or worldview by which they perceive the mystery of nature, land, spirituality and universe. So, merely relegating the tribal worldviews to antique, uncivilized, outdated etc. is indicative of contempt and monopoly over other culture, which is unbiblical. If a theology to be genuine and relevant then it must partake its culture and incarnate in its culture, and arise from its own cultural and religious ethos and experiences.

The Kukis, like other tribals, are also unique owing to their religious perceptions and practices. Even before the names, 'God' and 'Lord' of the Bible were heard, they, too, had their own concept of God-Lord in terms of *Chungmangpa* and *Noimangpa,* which share close affinity with the God and Lord of the Bible. An indigenous or a home-grown understanding of the gospel is felt urgent so the Christian religion or faith may be seen as nothing new or foreign to the Kukis but a sheer continuation of their unrealized Christ that was in their primal religion just as Messiah was for the Jews and the Logos for the Greek. Therefore, what is found at the present trend of the Kuki community is that the basis of their philosophical and spiritual foundation of their life such as custom-culture, social ethics, myths, folktales, religious symbols and images that have been largely trivialized since the advent of Christianity, should be rejuvenated. Therefore, in light of this, attempts have been made to relook and culturally interpret the gospel of Christ in order to have meaningful dialogue and greater impact upon the lives of the cultured people.

---

[12] R.H.S. Boyd, *An Introduction,* 328.

Chapter 1

Historical-Cultural Context and Theological Thoughts of C.S. Song towards Theology of Cultures

1.1. Life and Theological Background of C.S. Song

Choan-Seng Song was born in 1929. He is a Distinguished Professor Emeritus of Theology and Asian Cultures at the Pacific School of Religion and acting minister at the Formosan United Methodist Church in San Leandro, California. Song was also the principal of Tainan Theological College (1965-70) and later, President of the World Alliance of Reformed Churches (1977-2004).[1] In 1976-77, he served as Visiting Professor at Princeton Theological Seminary. He has also served as Director of Study for the World Alliance; and Associate Director of the Faith and Order Commission of the World Council of Churches, Geneva.[2] He is also Regional Professor of

[1] "C.S. Song," http://en.wikipedia.org/wiki/C._S._Song—cached (18 Aug. 2011).

[2] James Wu, "Song (,) Choan. Seng.," edited by Darek, people.bu.edu/wildman/bce/song.htm—cached similar (18 Aug. 2011).

Theology at the South East Asia Graduate School of Theology in Singapore and external examiner for the China University of Hong Kong.[3] He is also currently a visiting professor of School of Theology in Chang Jung Christian University, and also teaching part time at Yushan Theological College and Seminary. He is also a writer of many books on contextual theologies and story theology. He served as the first Dean of PTCA.[4] Due to political pressure, Song lives in exile and is unable to serve his Taiwanese people. Although he lives outside of his country, his theologies are developed through Asian background.[5] He has two daughters, Ju-Ping and Ju-Ying and his wife Mei-man are very supportive in his theological ministry especially in the field of writing.[6] He graduated in Philosophy from the National Tainan University (1950-54) and received his B.D. from New College at the University of Edinburgh (1955-58). He received his Ph.D. from the Union Theological Seminary, New York in 1965. Before joining the WCC, he taught Systematic Theology and served as the Principal of Tainan Theological College.[7] Henceforth we shall move towards his formative years in the field of theology.

1.2. Formative Factors of C.S. Song

Song delineates himself to have influenced by different theologians and scholars especially eminent theologians from Union Theological Seminary, New York such as Paul Tillich, Paul Lehman, D.D. Wiliams, Karl Barth, Oscar Cullmann and Baumgartner in Basel, Switzerland. He also came under the influence of Professor Norman Porteous, professor of Old Testament at New College, Edinburgh University and Professor James Muilenburg, professor of Old Testament at Union Theological Seminary in New York. His doctoral dissertation on the "Concepts of Revelation and Religion in the Theologies of Karl

---

[3] C.S. Song, "Christian Theology: Towards an Asian Reconstruction," www.religion-online.org/showarticle.asp? Title=128-cached similar (18 Aug. 2011).

[4] C.S. Song, "Doing Theologies with Stories: Theological Education, Where Do We Go From Here?" in *The Journal of Theologies and Cultures: Interreligious Education*, Vol. 10, (2011): 7.

[5] S. Batumalai, *An Introduction,* 72.

[6] S. Batumalai, *An Introduction,* 60.

[7] S. Batumalai, *An Introduction,* 59-60.

Barth and Paul Tillich," under the guidance of Daniel Day Williams (Systematic Theology, Union, NY) has largely influenced in his initial stage.[8] Batumalai in his book entitled, *An Introduction to Asian Theology* aptly states that Song was influenced by K. Barth at his early stage.[9] In addition to this, even Song himself neatly encapsulates, "I was held captive by my Western theological mentors such as Karl Barth and Paul Tillich as well as T.F. Torrance, my teacher at New College, Edinburgh University, an influential Scotish..." He further delineates himself to have ventured into the quest of the nature and truth of Christian theology on his own and developed his own theology informed by stories. Stories especially stories from Asia and stories from Taiwan that enables him to develop theological methods and construct Christian faith and theology different from Western theologies.[10] According to James Wu, Song was deeply influenced by Dr. Shoki Coe's (Ng Chiong-Hui) idea of the "contextualization of theology." Another factor, which influences Song's theology, is the Liberation Theology that adopts Marx's criticism on religion and capitalism that emphasizes on human freedom and social justice. Song observes that Asian people have been victimized by the Western industrialization and modernization. The imported value system of technological and economic developments of the West with its colonialism, have replaced the original value system of Asia. Thus, create identity crises.[11] Through this new venture and exploration, he reads and interprets the Bible from the Asian eyes which poses different theology from the West.

1.3. Cultural Context of C.S. Song

Prior to embarking to the context of culture, it is equally important to look at the political scenario of Taiwan. As in most of the cases, politics has always been central aspect of shaping one's culture, so

[8] C.S. Song, "Theological Transpositions," in *Theologies and Cultures: Theological Transpositions,* 7/2 (December 2010): 11.

[9] S. Batumalai, *An Introduction,* 60.

[10] C.S. Song, "Theological Transposition," 12-13.

[11] James Wu, "Song (,) Choan. Seng," people.bu.edu/wwildman/bce/song.htm – Cached.

is true to Taiwanese context. Politics covers the whole gamut of socio-politico-economic and religious life. According to Ya-Tang Chuang, in its last 400 years of history the Taiwanese people have suffered under various different ruling authorities. Dutch colonial occupation lasted for 37 years (1624-1662), the Koxing Dynasty directly followed with 21 years of dictatorship (1662-1683), and then for more than 200 years (1683-1895), the Manchu's Dynasty treated the Taiwanese as a "People out of jurisdiction," and handed it over to Japan as an indemnity-territory after Sino-Japan war. Imperial Japan then ruled Taiwan for 50 years (1895-1945). After World War II, the China-Nationalist government (KMT) implemented one-party rule and martial law for more than 40 years.[12] The imperial attempted to "Noppon-nize" them. And the KMT indoctrinates the Taiwanese to believe that they are "Chinese," the descendants of the Dragon. Rulers of China also claimed that Taiwanese are Chinese, sharing the common language and the common race with themselves. The Taiwanese were taught by these alien authorities not to identify themselves as "Taiwanese." Up till now many Taiwanese are confused of their own identity, there is ambiguity of political identity and confusion of cultural identity.[13] Thus, the context tells us how Taiwan was under the rule of alien authorities. Although, this reflects the political side of how Taiwan was for 400 years or more under imperialism yet it simultaneously also reflects how they were culturally exploited because politically suppressed country is without any exception from its cultural degradation. In addition to this, Song also asserts that the colonial rule or rule by the cultural foreign power does not allow people to be masters of their own affairs and destiny. All they do is to exploit their people, treating them as a bundle of grass, valueless and insignificant, and not caring whether they live or die.[14] However, with the achievement of democracy in

---

[12] Ya-Tan Chuang, "Practing Contextual Theology in Contemporary Taiwan: An Enquiry into the Theological Method of Selected Contextual Theologians of Taiwan," in *JTCA the Journal of Theologies and Cultures in Asia,* 133.

[13] Ya-Tan Chuang, "Practing Contextual Theology...," 1387-38.

[14] Choan-Seng Song, "From Indigenous Stories to Indigenous Culture to Indigenous Christian Theology: Case of Taiwan," in *Theologies and Cultures, Church and Empire,* 2/1 (June 2005): 107.

Taiwan on the eve of the presidential election on March 20, 2004 alongside the inauguration of the President and Vice-president that took place on the 20th of May, 2004, marked another chapter in the history of democracy in Taiwan.[15] Thus, the people of Taiwan begin to assert their right of self-determination, of being "masters of their own affairs and destiny."[16] This new outlook within the democratic arena of life has given rise to affirmation of culture and self-identity.

1.3.1. Culture and Self-Identity

Needless to say, as Song pointed out, since the abolition of martial law in 1987, in all fairness he admits that Taiwan's economic growth is very much indebted to elections, as astonishingly large amount of money change hands at every election, stimulating economic growth. Despite the economic affluence in the country however, now the government's attention is also moving towards the indigenous culture. In light of this, Song states, "Now the indigenous government is firmly in place at long last, the development of indigenous culture becomes a task of the greatest urgency. Elections, big or small, although important parts of a nation's life, should not be the whole of it."[17] He observes that the future of democracy in Taiwan is closely bound up with development of indigenous culture. Song, looking at the political aspect of indigenous culture asserts that "if this is true of democracy in Taiwan, it is not less true of Christian theology."[18] As a matter of fact, Christianity in Taiwan is still a Western religion. He views indigenous culture as a vital part of indigenous religious culture. It holds the key to the development of indigenous political culture. The same thing is said of the development of indigenous Christian theology. He necessitates indigenous culture in order to develop indigenous Christianity and indigenous Christian theology.[19] Speaking from the perspective of Taiwan culture, Song asserts that there is no culture for Taiwanese people to be commonly held their

---

[15] Choan-Seng Song, "From Indigenous...," 103.

[16] Choan-Seng Song, "From Indigenous...," 107.

[17] Choan-Seng Song, "From Indigenous...," 108.

[18] Choan-Seng Song, "From Indigenous...," 108.

[19] Choan-Seng Song, "From Indigenous...," 108..

own, "that all we have are cultures either imposed on us by foreign rulers or imported from outside, especially from China. Many Taiwanese people are captive to what is called China sentiment."[20] Now the attempt which Song puts forward is, to get rid of this China sentiment whether right or wrong, eliminating not culture from China but their misguided China cultural sentiment in order for them to develop healthy appreciation of Taiwanese indigenous culture.[21] Song, while trying to get rid of this China cultural sentiment, he is not unaware of culture being a composite entity which is a mixture of different cultures from ancient time to the present day. Now the question with which Song deals is not whether there are foreign cultural elements but whether there is a native cultural ingenuity capable of creatively integrating them into the indigenous cultural forms and substance. Song still finds the need to internal interactions between Christianity and indigenous culture in Taiwan and in most of Asian countries.[22] Thus, from the above discussion, Taiwanese cultural context as Song has depicted can be said as in the making of self-identity, self-assertion and setting a distinct cultural identity of its own by incorporating foreign cultural elements.

1.4. Brief Discussion on Song's Theological Methodology

Song borrows his methodology from Latin American Liberation theology that adopts mainly from a Marxist critique on religion and capitalism. Song portrays the people of Asia as being victimized by a history of western imperialism, both colonially and culturally, which creates an identity crisis for Asian Christians. Hence, the

---

[20] Choan-Seng Song, "From Indigenous...," 109.

[21] Choan-Seng Song, "From Indigenous...," 109-110.

[22] For example, Ancient Greek culture, Roman culture, or near Eastern cultures, Chinese cultures, Japanese culture, all have developed out of different cultural ingredients. These cultures are, without exception, pluralistic. As such Taiwan is also without exception. These nations from early time have developed strong self-identity as independent nations both as individual and nation. "They are able to translate their sense of self-identity into creative force, nurturing their indigenous cultural element on the one hand and, on the other, absorbing and transforming foreign cultural elements to become part of their own indigenous culture." Choan-Seng Song, "From Indigenous...," 110-111.

task of Contextualization is found through liberation of these unjust circumstances and the reconstruction of a new identity for Asian Christians.[23] Song's theological construction is based on a synthesis of the liberation theology, the narrative theology, the biblical theology and the theology of cultures. Although Song has been struggling for liberation from the dominion of the Western theology, yet Western theological views and values still underlie his theological construction. Song takes the "Asian experience" a source for constructing an Asian Christian theology. In order to search for the existential meaning of the Asian people, Song penetrates and reinterprets the traditional Asian folk tales and the modern Asians' living stories with his "Third Eye."[24] Taking into account third eye theology, Song juxtaposes Asian stories with biblical stories, and interprets the Asian stories in correspondence with implementing of the "contextualization of theology."[25] As pointed out by Chen Nan-Jou, extracting from the book entitled *The Modern Theologians*, edited by David F. Ford, authored by George Gispert-Swech, "Asian Theology," says that Song's theological language is more imaginative than most theologians do. Song's theology is not only from the perspective of redemption, but also from the perspective of creation. His theological argument is that God's creation in fact is redemption, and the redemption is new creation. He also advocates "story theology." Doing theology by telling stories, Song makes theology as literatures such as stories and parables. Song's understanding is that "each theological formulation, be it that of a venerable church father or that of impressive German theology, is historically and culturally conditioned and must be appreciated and critiqued as such. It has no automatic claim to universal authority."[26]

---

[23] C.S. Song, en.wikipedia.org/wiki/C._S._Song—cached (18 Aug. 2011).

[24] The "Third Eye," a term derived from the Japanese Buddhism, is an eye seeing Christ with one's cultural experience. Christians in Asia should be trained to see Christ with their own experience. Seeing Christ through the Asian cultural experience invokes the spirituality of the Asian people.

[25] James WU, " Song (,) Choan .Seng," edited by Darek Mirand, people.bu.edu/wwildman/bce/song.htm—cached similar (18 Aug. 2011).

[26] Chen Nan-Jou, "Theology is a Disclosure of Life: C.S. Song's Theology in Focus," in *Theologies and Cultures*, 6/2 (December 2009): 10.

For Song, 'Jesus' Reign of God' is the criterion for tracing the footsteps of God. In view of this, Chen Nan-Jou states that Song proposes five stages towards a theological reconstruction. Stage one refers to a fundamental question such as 'Is God's salvation bound by the Christian Church?' Stage two refers to the story of Jesus as the story of the Reign of God, and through the Reign of God the story of Jesus is told as the story of God, and through it the story of God is told as the story of Jesus. The Reign of God plays a crucial part to know Jesus and to experience God. It is the key to unlock the mystery surrounding God. Stage three talks about stories of God's Reign in Asia. Stage four talks about Christian church returning to its faith and theology and look at it with the story of Jesus as the story of God's Reign and with the stories of people in Asia that reflects the story of God's Reign. Stage five is about to let the story of Jesus and stories from Asia inter-penetrate each other. Song discovers that by this theological approach "a theological space is also opened for the stories of Hebrew Scriptures. Stories from other parts of the world also come into play. Thus, a theological feast of stories takes place. The story of Jesus, stories from Asia, stories in Hebrew Scripture, and stories from the rest of the world, told as stories of God's Reign.[27]

Song also takes seriously theological transpositions as a basis to reformulate theological curriculum, and re-constructing theological education as a whole, in the post-modern world of the 21st century to make gospel relevant to Asian cultures. It is a transposition from theological traditions dominated by the churches and theologians of the West to a theology that deals with sources and experiences of people outside the West. This transposition is prompted by the re-discovery of stories ignored, suppressed and then removed from the Christian church and its theology.[28] In the succeeding section, theological transpositions will be discussed in detail.

---

[27] Chen Nan-Jou, "Theology is a Disclosure of Life...," 11.

[28] C.S. Song, "Theological Transpositions," in *Theologies and Cultures*, 7/2, (December 2010): 10.

1.5. Moving Towards his Theology of Cultures

Song, prior to the discussion on theology of cultures, has made an enormous attempt to understand first a different sets of Christian doctrine and fundamental teachings such as incarnation, creation, redemption, Jesus, Christ, messenger and message. Henceforth, he gradually moves towards theology of cultures based on an already existing traditional theologies and in many cases, while attempting to look at the Christian doctrines and basic teachings from the creation perspective, he comes out with the reversal of the traditional theology. Thus, some of his theological movement towards theology of cultures will be assessed accordingly.

1.5.1. An Attempt to Formulate Theology of Incarnation

Song explicitly describes incarnation in the perspective of the present—present is neither the past nor the future; it is the consummation of the past and the threshold to the future. For him human being is bound to such a present. He is against to the concept of transcendence, which according to him is opposed to historical being because he conceives transcendence of one's self means one becomes a non-historical being thereby, transcendence implies either self-deception or naïve optimism. He further affirms that the message of Christian Bible is not emancipation from limitation and finiteness, but from sin of pride.[29] The theology of incarnation— perspective of present is emerged out of the church's tendency to fall back on the past largely in a situation where the church is not being able to cope with the mysterious character of the present. Song sees the past provides comfortable terms of reference whenever the church is challenged into taking its own theological and ethical stand.[30] Song

[29] Choan-Seng Song, "Theology of the Incarnation," in *Asian Voices in Christian Theology*, edited and with an Introduction by Gerald H. Anderson (New York: Orbis Books, 1976), 155.

[30] Furthermore, Song also notices the church indulging in speculation about the future which never threatens it with existential decision. In all its effort the present is brushed aside in order for the past to be transplanted to the future. In this framework of past and future of the church's, the present is not held. Thus, this leads to the rejection of Jesus Christ as the Lord here and now. Over to this view, Song clarifies that "the theology anchored in the present as the perspective

observes that the incarnation is this present, not as a principle to be followed, but as perspective—that is, as dynamic force giving birth to new moments in the midst of the old. As such it is an event, or the event, in that something happens when it interferes with the mundane. Song equates incarnation with eternally present which is powerful creative force, by this powerful creative force, and the past is translated to the future, darkness yields to glory, despair gives way to hope, and death conquered. This incarnational event comes into being when the past and the future are brought into the focus of the incarnation.[31] Theology of incarnation is the interaction between truths scattered in God's creation and the Truth revealed in Jesus Christ. It is the arena where the strayed truths in human history and culture are once again united with the Truth which is in Jesus Christ.[32]

Song also undertakes incarnational theology from the perspective of God's mission of enfleshment reflected in the book *Christian Mission in Reconstruction.* Song states that God's mission of enfleshment in Jesus Christ is God becoming what he is not. This entails the risk of God losing His own identity. It is paradoxical to say that God is becoming no longer God. However for Song, this miracle of enfleshment does not result in God forfeiting His identity as Creator and Redeemer. On the contrary, Song says, "By becoming other than what He is, namely, by becoming present and manifest in Jesus Christ, He has revealed Himself as what He truly is. This is the heart of the paradox of Christian faith."[33] From the point of mission of enfleshment, Song observes the task of Christian mission is not to Christianize the world but to make contribution to the renewal of civilizations deeply rooted in other religions. It sounds shocking yet it is not a betrayal of Christian faith. He reiterates "the chief task of Christian mission is to let the faith in Jesus Christ become the

---

giving meaning to the past and holding up hope for the future is the theology of the incarnation—the theology which reckons with the immediate presence of the Eternal One in the midst of temporal and transient." Choan-Seng Song, "Theology of the Incarnation," 156.

[31] Choan-Seng Song, "Theology of the Incarnation," 156.

[32] Choan-Seng Song, "Theology of the Incarnation," 157.

[33] Choan-Seng Song, *Christian Mission,* 55.

germinal element which enables civilization to be renewed as witness to the glory of God's creation and manifestation of the presence of God as Saviour in the world."[34] Owing to this concept of incarnation as conceived, Song does not necessitate converting people into the fold of Christian community and integrating them into the religious structure of the church.[35] Song stands for Christ-centered mission over the church-centered mission. Christ centered mission for Song means, Jesus Christ is at the intersection of the divine dimension and the human dimension at every stage of history from creation to incarnation. Therefore, in Jesus Christ God saturates the whole history of human beings and the world.[36] Further Song says that Christ-centered mission defines the nature and function of the church and therefore, the church is an event rather than an organization, fellowship rather than church order.[37]

1.5.2. Contextualization of Theology in Asian Terms

Incarnational theology is a basis for Song from which he is further led to a theology of contextualization. In fact Song's books have no less concentration on theology of incarnation and contextualization. Batumalai has rightly pointed out that Song sees Christ's incarnation as God taking history seriously to which the mission of enfleshment has immense implications for the process of contextualization.[38] Song emphatically demands the need for doing theology with Asian resources. He sees the difficulty to continue singing somebody else's theological tune. He advocates finding our own theological voice because our own cultures, religions, and histories are unrelated to the Christianity which is brought from the West because of the stereotyped theological and missiological pronouncements on our cultural, religious and historical realities made by our mentors in the West, if not entirely fallacious, were invalid and misleading and are "genetically" incapable of knowing what it means to live in the world

[34] Choan-Seng Song, *Christian Mission,* 57.

[35] Choan-Seng Song, *Christian Mission,* 55.

[36] Choan-Seng Song, *Christian Mission,* 61.

[37] Choan-Seng Song, *Christian Mission,* 63.

[38] S. Batumalai, *An Introduction,* 66.

of Buddhist culture, Hindu culture or Confucian culture.[39] Thus, Song in his attempt to contextualize he starts with Asian resources such as folk literatures and stories, histories, religions, symbols and images and cultures of Asia.[40]

1.5.3. Theological Transposition

Simply put it, for Song, theological transposition is a "transposition from theological traditions dominated by the churches and theologians of the West to a theology that deals with sources and experiences of people outside the West."[41] Hence, we shall briefly assess Song's theological transposition in which he painstakingly labours to let the gospel incarnate in one's own culture without any intervention of the Western theology.

1.5.3.1. Transposition from Israel to Asia

One of the earliest articles which he wrote to start his theological transposition is entitled "From Israel to Asia." He conceives ancient Israel as the prototype of Christian faith, when failed, Christianity succeeded. In other words, he states, Christianity is "Christianized" Israel. The Hebrew Bible was christened as the Old Testament and God's covenant with Israel was superseded as an "old" covenant by Christianity as the new covenant. God gave promises to Israel to be fulfilled in Christianity. Israel has been Christianized Israel that was brought to Asia and taught in Asian Seminaries. Thus he calls Christianity as a second Israel, a true Israel, but an Israel packaged in the West.[42] Therefore, the search for a direct interaction between Israel and Asia without any intervention of the West is sought in this theological enterprise.

---

[39] Choan Seng (C.S.), "Christian Theology: Asian Way," in *Doing Theology with Asian Resources: Theology and Cultures*, Vol. II (np: ATESEA, 1995), 22.

[40] Choan Seng (C.S.), "Christian Theology...," 25-30.

[41] C.S. Song, "Theological Transpositions," 10.

[42] C.S. Song, "Theological Transpositions," 13.

1.5.3.2. Transposition from Redemption to Creation

Song states that transposition from Israel to Asia leads him to the next fundamental theological transposition i.e. from redemption to creation. He realizes that the theological framework developed by Western theologians do not work when the attention is turned to Asia from Israel. He critiques Western theologians because of their teaching about creation being narrowed down steadily to Christ and from Christ extends out to a new creation, forming what they call 'salvation history.' For him it is a "West-centric" interpretation of history and at the same time "West-Christianity-centric" interpretation of Christ.[43] Song notices that Christian teachings and doctrines miss out the importance of creation to a large amount. He observes the emphasis on redemption as one-sided. Song's conviction is that outside the Christian church, Asian context is very different. In the sense, creation or nature plays a dominant part in people's life in Asia. He resonates, "Getting out of bed in the morning, one is greeted by nature. Lunar calendar is meticulously followed by most people, urban or rural, particularly by farmers as they calculate sowing times and harvesting times...people are very aware that they live at the mercy of nature, depending upon heaven for their livelihood. Nature or creation is part and parcel of their lives."[44] Thus, for Song, redemption is meaningless without nature or creation that has been turned down by the Western theology.

1.5.3.3. Transposition from Absolute to Relational

In regard to this approach, Song tends to avoid the claim of Absoluteness in any religion. For him, claiming to be absolute for what one believes, one in fact commits logical fallacy and factual error. He stresses that the claim of being absolute has not allowed to be compared with others. It avoids comparison with other things thereby no knowledge of it. It is a rejection of all other claims to absoluteness. This is how "an absolute religion" comes into being. He articulates, "An absolute religion inevitably is a militant religion

---

[43] C.S. Song, "Theological Transpositions," 17.

[44] C.S. Song, "Theological Transpositions," 18-19.

trying to subject other religions or suppress them."[45] Thus, Song is convinced of the paradigm shift of transposition from absolute to relational, relativizes Christian claim to absoluteness and compels Christians and theologians to look at cultures and religions other than those of Christianity in their own light.[46] Thus, for him being relational is a gateway for mutual enrichment in a religiously plural world and to avoid absolutism that is theological fallacy.

1.5.3.4. Transposition from Christ to Jesus

This is another key transposition he has made in faith and theology. He asserts, "For me, transposition from Christ to Jesus finally enables me to make a decisive breakthrough in the Western formulation of faith and theology."[47] In this transposition, Song, in fact, reverses the Western theological formulation of 'Jesus to Christ' into 'Christ to Jesus.' According to him there are many Christs, Christs created by the Orthodox Church, the Roman Catholic Church and Protestant Churches of many hues and colours, each claiming to bring the authentic Christ.[48] In view of this, there is a question like, 'whose Christ represents the Jesus who walked the earth two thousand years ago in Palestine. This is the place where each church claims the authenticity of their own denominational based gospel, which has given rise to serious questions about Christian faith.

In fact, Song sees the image of Christ so much distorted by different churches so that it is almost impossible to grasp the true image of Christ. He sees that the Christ brought to South Africa was a white Christ, the Christ of the oppressors. The Christ of the South Africans was a black Christ, the Christ of the oppressed. It is Christ against Christ. A conflict between powerful Christ and powerless Christ takes place in South Africa.[49]

Transposing Christ to Jesus, Song himself faces difficulty, and sees the risk involved in because there are so many layers to peel off

---

[45] C.S. Song, "Theological Transpositions," 20.

[46] C.S. Song, "Theological Transpositions," 22.

[47] C.S. Song, "Theological Transpositions," 22.

[48] C.S. Song, "Theological Transpositions," 22.

[49] C.S. Song, "Theological Transpositions," 23.

before one could reach the core called Jesus. He says that even when you think you reach that core, it may turn to be your Christ, not Jesus.[50] He himself confesses honestly that Jesus to whom he has transposed may not be the real Jesus. He may be closer to Jesus, but it still has Christ. What makes his effort difficult is that there are very few historical accounts of Jesus, the fact considered is that historical record of some persons in his time and before his time can be a whole lot richer. Here he presumes of some doubt that Christians tend to overestimate Jesus' fame in his time or the doctrine of atonement that the church developed which made him more than a life-sized Christ. The veneration of him as the second person in the Trinity might have minimized his humanity and maximized his divinity.[51] Thus, the attempt in this transposition is to uncover the humanness of Jesus so that the humanity of Jesus may be culturally conceived in a real sense of life so that it gives values and meaning of life amidst the oppression and struggle for life.

1.5.3.5.. Transposition from Messenger to Message

Song necessitates that once the transposition from Christ to Jesus has been made, another methodological transposition has to be undertaken i.e. transposition from messenger to message. He echoes that Christology as that is known has been the axis around which almost all Christian teachings and doctrines are developed and evolved, especially the Christology emerged out from the famous Nicene Creed, which has shaped and dominated the faith and theology of the Christian churches from the 4th century to the 21st century.[52] Thus, he sees Christ as God that has remained to this day; as a result this has become the criterion of biblical interpretation and theological construction, ruling out other biblical hermeneutics and theological formulations.[53] However, Song's main concern

---

[50] C.S. Song, "Theological Transpositions," 23.

[51] C.S. Song, "Theological Transpositions," 24.

[52] C.S. Song, "Theological Transposition," 25-26.

[53] Song observes Christ is the heart of the Nicene Creed, even God and the Spirit, found its way into the creed to support the Christology of the church of the early church early centuries. He stresses that the Christology summed up in the

is not to oppose the time-honoured Nicene Creed, but to know whether it reflected Jesus of Nazareth, Jesus the son of Mary and Joseph, Jesus who in his short public ministry lived, struggled and eventually crucified on the cross. He is of the view that neither the Christology of the Nicene Creed nor the Christology of the churches after Nicene Creed, nor the churches outside the West, reflected that Jesus. He views that what most Christians have been confessing is Jesus reconstructed by the Nicene Creed and the Churches.[54] On the contrary, he has made an attempt to reverse the procedure, transposing from the message to the message of the messenger. In this case, he refers the message as Jesus' rule (reign) of God. He is convinced to almost 80% of Jesus' message is related to the rule of God. He takes precious little historical account of Jesus as a basis to start with the work i.e. his message of God's rule back to his person as Jesus, that is, from his message to his person.[55] This message is none other than the reign of God. Jesus' message is all about the reign of God, this reign of God is unconditionally permeated in all cultures irrespective Christian or non-Christian religions.

1.5.4. Creation and Universal Mission of God to all Nations

As has been already dealt, for Song, creation and redemption are inseparably linked. However, what the traditional and rest of the Church's theologies often overlook is creation over redemption. Therefore, Song points out that redemption is meaningless without nature or creation especially insofar Asian context is concerned.[56] He understands God as a God of creation and redemption, failure to see two aspects from the view point of the same coin, would mean incomplete and merely one-sided view of salvific history of the West. Batumalai notices that for Song, "God moves on in compassion. We have no alternatives but to move on with God. This God creates,

---

Creed by the early church is deification of Jesus as Christ, the Son of God, of the same substance of God. C.S. Song, "Theological Transposition," 26.

[54] C.S. Song, "Theological Transposition," 26.

[55] C.S. Song, "Theological Transposition," 26.

[56] C.S. Song, "Theological Transpositions," 19.

redeems, and recreates a family and a human community."[57] The Asian culture is one of the creatures that belong to God's universal creation. In fact over to his view on creation has a direct implication to theology of cultures. Therefore, Song believes that God's redemptive love must have revealed in the Asian cultures as well.[58] Thomas also shares similar views in his statement that a lopsided anthropology of the evangelical-pietistic tradition of his church needs to be corrected at the theological and anthropological levels. He believes that incarnation is the continuation of Creation.[59]

Song in his book, *The Compassionate God*, points out radically that the traditional theology either from the Jewish framework of God's redemptive history to the Western theology or the East is a straight-line God and a straight-line theology.[60] On the contrary, Song proposes God's Universal love as a basis to understand God's boundless acts and intervention in the multi-religious context. Love for Song, is a most simple and yet most powerful thing. It brings lives into being, sustains them, nourishes and enriches them. Love is the Word through which God comes to us and we to God. "God is love," which he has quoted from I John 4:8. He is of the view that to turn God into a straight-line God is to caricature God.[61] Song describes love as not a geometrical concept, it cannot be measured by ruler, it cannot be weighed on a balance, it cannot be straightened out by a line but love is round, not a straight, it does not penetrate space like a straight line but fills it and saturates. It is not a linear but

---

[57] S. Batumalai, *An Introduction to Asian Theology...*, 63.

[58] C.S. Song, *people.bu.edu/wwildman/bce/song.htm* - Cached HYPERLINK "http://www.google.co.in/search?hl=en&client=firefox-a&hs=OLW&rls=org.mozilla:en-US:official&channel=s&biw=1526&bih=721&q=related:people.bu.edu/wwildman/bce/song.htm+c.s.song&tbo=1&sa=X&ei=vghWTqLtHIWnrAeqr_HPCg&ved=0CDAQHzAC"Similar (18th Aug. 2011).

[59] T. M. Philip, *The Encounter Between Theology and Ideology: An Exploration into the Communicative Theology of M .M. Thomas* (Madras: The Christian Literature Society, 1986), 38.

[60] This approach of God's redemptive act does not allow any interference which is logically ordered such as creation, the fall, the election of Israel, Jesus Christ, the Church as the new Israel and final fulfillment, follow one after the other.

[61] Choan-Seng Song, *The Compassionate God*, 25.

a concentrical movement.[62] Reflecting on the Deutronomic theology of history with its centrism of Israel, Song states, "A transposition from the Israel—centered view of history that regards other nations as constructive parts of God's design of history is required for a more realistic perception of God's work in the world. Such new theology of history contains a tacit admission that Israel alone cannot explain world history."[63] Thus, Song is clear in his approach that religious centrism of Israel as a theology of militant is replaced by a theology of a compassionate God, a humble theology of a suffering God. God who is already defined within the framework of Judaic-Christian concept cannot be final and universal because God cannot be defined by our mere religious and social common sense.[64] Thus, for Song, on the basis of God's universal love he regards the salvation history of the Bible as a pattern, not a norm, that God manifests God's love toward the human beings in the cultures.

1.6. Evaluation of Song's Theological Thoughts

In a way different theologians have assessed Song is varied: Chen Nan-Jou remarks that Song's theology centres on life therefore, it is just opposite to traditional systematic theology. "Song's theology crosses the boundary of the traditional theology. He advocates the interdisciplinary integration in theological education. Thus Song's theology is Biblical hermeneutics, theology of mission, socio-political ethics, and theological studies of life and death."[65]

However, despite Song's strenuous effort to be wholly independent of traditional theology, Batumalai points out that there is a tendency for Song and other theologians to return to Western resources.[66] Anri Morimoto has commented that Song seems at times very harsh and critical for the need to be theologically independent of the Western heritage. He further points out that in his well-known book *Jesus the Crucified People*, Song charges the entire history of

---

[62] Choan-Seng Song, *The Compassionate God,* 26.

[63] Choan-Seng Song, *The Compassionate God,* 49.

[64] Choan-Seng Song, *The Compassionate God,* 49.

[65] Chen Nan-Jou, "Theoloy is a Disclosure of Life,"19.

[66] S. Batumalai, *An Introduction,* 73.

Western theology, beginning from St. Paul, as the chief culprit of theologizing, for turning the simple Gospel that Jesus proclaimed into an abstract system that has no connection to real life.[67] Over to this what Anri Morimoto points out is right that the third eye is to complement the two eyes, not replacing the two altogether, it is difficult to reform and rebuild our tradition from scratch but it can only be built our tradition on top of what already is.[68] However, his attempts to get rid of western theological hegemony have been such an eye opening in the theological domains for Asians.

According to Song, the transpositional theology is prerequisite to the communication of the Christian gospel to the Third World. He insists on the changeability of the gospel by taking an example of God's incarnation through Jesus Christ in us all. He strongly propagates that the gospel can come in any shape and in any colour and through theological transposition the gospel incarnate into the Asian soil and deals with Asian sources—cultural resources and experiences. Therefore, Song denounces any claim of absoluteness of theological dictum. Rather he prefers to use 'relational' instead of considering Christian doctrine and teaching of God as a norm to which all religions should plunge. At this point, Song is at ease in the claim for the uniqueness of every religious teaching. Thus, he feels the need for contextualization; the interaction between the biblical stories and people's live stories and experiences in Asia. When Christian theology is deeply rooted in Asian soil, i.e. cultures, theological interaction will be made possible. It would not be incorrect to say that Song's theology of incarnation has furthered him to theology of transposition and then to theology of cultures.

While emphasizing on the importance of cultures, Song also argues that God is God of all nations. God is involved in the life and history of the nations beyond the orbit of the Christian church.[69] Based on the concept of the universality of God, Song finds the

---

[67] Anri Morimoto, "Theology that Breaths Asia: The Lasting Contribution to the Global Christian Community," in *Theologies and Cultures: Theological Transposition,* 70.

[68] Anri Morimoto, "Theology that Breaths...,"70-71.

[69] Choan –Sens Song, *The Compassionate God,* 83.

centrism in the traditional theology as the major problem that makes Christians blind at other religious culture the fact that God is at work in other persons of all sorts and conditions.[70] He observes that centrism of traditional Christian theology devalues God's saving activity working outside the sacred history of Israel and the Church. The traditional theology has reduced the value of women, blacks and those of other cultures and faiths. Song logically argues that the word non-Christian is discriminatory. Therefore he says, "We are what we are, not what we-are-not. We are not non-apes, but human beings. Our Buddhist and Hindu friends are Buddhist and Hindu, not non-Christians. They do not find their identity in relation to Christians; they find it within their heritage because of their faith, on their own."[71] This statement indicates in a way Song is seriously taking the context of the people, their history, cultures and religions. He identifies God's presence at work in every race and culture and beyond Christian experiences. Thus, churches would not require demolishing of one's religious heritage. To this end, we have many biblical evidences about God's concerns and involvements in other nations other than Israel. To mention few, God's active participation for building nation is evidenced by Sodom and Gomorrah when He wanted to compromise with the cities from destruction if ever He could find a righteous person in the countdown series. God wanted to save Nineveh because He loved the people, so He sent Jonah to avoid the impending predicament that would befall on them by repenting from their sins. God saved the Egyptians through Joseph, the governor, only next to King. History of Israel is a history of God's compassionate movements over ancient communities irrespective of religion, culture and race.

1.7. Conclusion

Having dealt with Song's theological thoughts that move towards theology of cultures, he makes us rethink some of the very basic concept about God, Christ, creation, redemption, incarnation and

---

[70] Choan –Sens Song, *The Compassionate God,*132

[71] Choan-Seng Song, *The Compassionate God: A Exercise in the Theology of Transposition* (London: SCM Press Ltd., 1982), 64.

liberation from the perspective of theological transposition. In brief it can be said that Song's theology is an attempt to liberate from the domination of Western theology while trying to construct a theology viable of its own from the Asian cultural context. Indeed, Song's theology of incarnation, contextualization of theology in Asian terms, theological transposition, creation and universal mission of God to all nations are focused towards recognition of one's own culture—its uniqueness, potentiality and capability of conceiving God's redemptive work in every culture and nation. In other words, it is intrinsically linked with the emphasis of cultural importance.

In his theological transposition, Christians are challenged to have a broader view of God's saving activities in the Third World cultures, Asia. There is no doubt that God's saving activity continues in the lives of all people and nations. However, this also demands us to observe carefully the sign of God's saving activity among the majority of the world's populations. For Song, the Reign of God happens in the Christian Bible is simultaneously happens in the lives of the people all over the world. The way he treats biblical concept of creation and redemption has an immense implication for doing Christian theology in Asian context where creation or nature plays a vital role in the lives of Asian people and culture. Indeed his approach feels us obligatory to make gospel meaningful and relevant to Asian context where in Asia, creation or nature is part and parcel of their lives. On the contrary, the Western theology that emphasizes on the salvific act of God merely rules out, to use Song's word, "Asian spirituality," in its total sense. Song's theology of incarnation or enfleshment has an immense implication for the Asian people in general and the Kukis in particular who struggle for their life in the midst of chaos, socio-political injustice, cultural decay, corruption, sufferings and oppressions. In the light of Song's critique of theology against the Asian theology and church's canon and dogma garbed in Western costume, like most of the tribal churches in the North East, especially Christianity among the Kukis, is also without exception. Many of the Kuki cultural elements were treated as anti-Christian elements thereby, either discarded or demeaned. Hence, there is need for change of theological methodology.

Chapter 2

C.S. Song's Theology of Cultures in Asian Context

2.1. Introduction

In order to overcome the theological treatment on cultures by the West, Song has made an attempt to understand cultures from Asian perspective that are characterized by its inclusivity. The theological treatment on cultures by the West is dichotomizing into two separate entities; either gospel has nothing to do with people's cultures or vice versa. There seems to be an exclusive claim for Christian culture from the West, while relegating others' as unchristian. Discarding of cultural elements and values of the tribals by the early missionaries as such is indicative. It is due to their frown attitude towards the tribal cultures developed from their theological worldview of science and metaphysics. Thus, against the backdrop of this understanding, Song's understanding of cultures is assessed in relation to Christian theology from Asian context.

2.2. Different Definitions and Explanations of Culture

The *New Webster Encyclopaedia Dictionary* defines culture as *cultum* from *colo,* a Latin word which means to till; cultivation; intellectual development; improvement by mental or physical training; education; the way of life, refinement of people, to grow in a prepared medium etc.[1] Since this is a very basic understanding of culture, it has no point of contact culture with religion. Amalorpavadass defines, "Culture is a complex reality but an integrated, interacting and integrating dynamic whole: it consists of the following constitutive elements: Common world vision, view of life or outlook on life, common goals, common values and common meaning (value-system and meaning-systems, ideology), common thinking conditioned by common environment and common traditions, common behaviour patterns, with a whole gamut of organized relationships and organized way of living, a consciousness of life, a common aesthetic outlook and a capacity for a characteristically common action. It includes also a transcendent and in-depth dimension: religion and philosophy, spirituality and mysticism."[2]

A more interesting and one of the most noted American theologians, from theological approach by H Richard Niebuhr, in his book *Christ and Culture,* defines culture as "artificial, secondary environment which man (sic) superimposes on the natural. It comprises language, habits, ideas, beliefs, customs, and values. Since human beings are inextricably bound up with society, "it is always social." Second understanding of culture "is human achievement." "Culture is the work of men's (sic) mind and hands...hence it includes speech education, tradition, myth, science, art, philosophy, government, law, rite, beliefs, inventions, technologies."[3] However, Song views that the typology of the relationship between Christianity

---

[1] "Culture," in *The New Webster Encyclopaedia Dictionary of the English language Including A Dictionary of Synonyms and Twelve Supplementary Reference Sections*, edited Virginia S. Thatcher et al., (Chicago: Consolidated Book Publishers, n.d.), 209.

[2] Swami Amalorpavadass, *Theological Reflections on Inculturation* (Mysore: Anjali Ashram, n.d.), 13.

[3] H. Richard Niebuhr, *Christ and Culture* (New York: Harpers & Brothers, 1951), 32-33.

and culture developed by Richard Niebuhr has been too readily applied to Asian situations to which he was not addressing himself. This has resulted into polarization of Christian experience and cultural identity, setting former against the latter.[4] Ya-Tang Chuang further points out that Song finds contradiction on Niebuhr's classification of Christ and Culture into five types such as *Christ against culture, the Christ of culture, Christ above culture, Christ and culture in Paradox*, and *Christ the transformer of culture*. Song's view on Niebuhr's five typology does not fit Jesus' dealing with Jewish culture, for he did not pose himself as "against, for, above, or in paradox with" his own culture in its entirety nor did Jesus aim at transforming it. Rather Jesus sought to bring out the best in the religious culture of his day and urged to reconstruct the community based on it. The reconstruction community that he envisioned is the reign of God.[5] Hence, with this prelude of Song's understanding of cultures, a further cogent and logical approach of cultures will be assessed from different perspectives.

2.3. Song's Understanding of Cultures in Relation to Christian Theology

As cited by Ya-Tang Chuang, Song elaborates culture in this way:

> Culture by itself is an empty concept. Without concrete referents culture is a meaningless word. Basically, culture is a derivative term, a term that comes alive and breaths with meaning only when it gets related to something other than itself. Culture is not a subject-word but a predicate-word. It is predicated on something else. It cannot dictate others but is dictated by other. It cannot designate things, but is designated by them. It is to use a metaphor familiar to us, a tire before it is inflated with air. A tire with no air is useless. It cannot make a bicycle, a car or a bus, run. To continue the metaphor of fire and air, in cultures

[4] Choan Seng (C.S), "Christian Theology: An Asian Way," 31.

[5] Ya-Tang Chuang, "Gospel and Culture in the Theology of C.S. Song...," 5.

> and religions we are not discussing them merely as a theological problem but as life-and-death matters related to our daily lives.[6]

A term culture as Song understood is a derivative term derives from the affairs of human beings. In true sense, it is human beings that precede culture. In brief, culture is evolved out of human affairs and activities. Culture exists only in relation to human beings; therefore, culture has to do with human beings in their relationship with one another and environment. Theologically, what is important is to deal with human beings, talk about the people in a particular culture through their own respective cultural thought forms and patterns not just negating them as godless and anti-Christian.

2.3.1. Intrinsic Relations between Cultures and Christian Theology

Song emphatically states, "There is no such thing as a theology immune from cultural and historical influences. Theology is culturally and historically not neutral. A neutral theology is a homeless theology. It does not belong anywhere. There really begins in earnest when it identifies its home and discovers its belonging."[7] In light of this understanding, Song approaches culture in broad sense of explicit and implicit expressions of human activities that constitute life and history. Related to this, he also stresses that theology is also a human activity derived from divine initiatives within the world. Thus, theology or Christianity for this matter has a lot more in common with other areas of human cultural and historical activities. Song in this matter has brought out practical example from a historical perspective: "church architect is a good example," says Song. For instance, the history, theology, and piety of the Christian church are enshrined in the architecture of churches and cathedrals throughout Europe. "The best in human perception of beauty, the noblest in human effort to get at the root of the mystery that surrounds human life, and perhaps the worst fear that arises out of the realization of the

---

[6] Ya-Tang Chuang, "Gospel and Cultures in the Theology of C.S. Song," in *JTCA: The Journal of Theologies and Cultures in Asia*, 6 (2007): 7.

[7] C.S. Song, *Tell Us Our Names; Story Theology From Asian Perspective* (New York: Orbis Books, 1989), 11.

human finiteness, are all brought to an amazing confluence in the construction of the European cathedral. It is no exaggeration to say that every aspect of human talent was tapped, every facet of human imagination was exploited in its construction."[8] Thus, either Chinese or other Asian cultures and histories are inherently theological. Song has put it very sharply that "Our theological home is the culture and history of which we are a part by birth and association. This is where our theology must be done. Our theology in Asia has been a homeless theology because we have forsworn our home. But our theological wanderings in alien homes are coming to an end."[9] With the discovery of theological roots, now in Asian lands, struggle for human rights are taking place, aspiration for freedom and assertion of political right keeps taking place. This has been possible only when our Christian theology is retrieved to Asian cultures. On the basis of this intrinsic relation between theology and cultures, Song moves on towards the root of an indigenous culture so that it becomes indigenously Christian theology by drawing its theological sources from it.

2.3.2. Starting with Indigenous Popular Culture

After having confirmed the inseparable relationships between theology and cultures, and viewing culture as nothing but "us" human beings, Song attempts to retrieve the indigenous popular culture as a starting point for Christian theology. According to Song, indigenous popular culture is a people's culture, which Christianity

---

[8] All these artistic expressions of Christian faith, says Song, are unthinkable without the cultural and historical traditions of Europe. On the basis of this enlightening example, Song is disappointed to think of culture unrelated to Christian theology, more importantly, the assumption that only the culture deeply influenced by Christianity can have a legitimate place in Christian theology. Therefore, a further stress is made by Song from incarnational perspective, although God took human form in a particular Jewish context, lived and died, but God's relationship with that culture and history could not have been closer. Implicit in such discussion is God's relationship with Chinese culture and history or Asian cultures and histories. They are not without God; it is not godless culture and history. Even the culture and history formed under atheistic political systems is not godless. C.S. Song, *Tell Us Our Names,* 11.

[9] C.S. Song, *Tell Us Our Names,* 12.

tends to scorn, dissociating from it and to esteem elite culture, associating with it. This proved to be detrimental to the development of indigenous Christian theology. In describing what indigenous popular culture really is, Song sees that every movement one makes and every action one takes person's thoughts and ideas, including one's religious beliefs, are closely related to the culture into which one is born. This culture, into which one is born acquired by status and exerting, is what he means by indigenous popular culture, in the sense of being rooted in one's being or in one's DNA.[10] Song elaborates what really indigenous popular culture is;

> Indigenous popular culture, or indigenous people's culture, is the culture of clothing, food, shelter and means of movement," four essential requirements of the people. From these four essential requirements or needs, people's culture has evolved and developed, and continues to evolve and develop. The basic need to cover the body from heat and cold evolves and develops dress industry; there is thus history of dress industry. Simple need for food evolves and develops into culinary arts; there is thus history of culinary arts. Primitive need to have a roof over one's head evolves and develops into architecture; there is thus history of architecture. Daily need for movement evolves and develops into more and more sophisticated means of travel and rapid systems of communications; there is thus history of human movements that so all the way back tens and hundreds of thousands years back.[11]

---

[10] Choan-Seng Song, "From Indigenous Stories…," 111-112.

[11] Further explication of indigenous popular culture: This elementary meaning of indigenous popular culture makes us realize that Christianity has committed a fundamental mistake in Asia and Africa as it intentionally separates itself from indigenous popular culture. Having deprived itself of its roots in indigenous popular culture, indigenous Christian theology has little chance to come alive. It fails to strike the chord with people's hearts and minds, as it merely repeats the religious and theological legacies it has inherited from the West. Religion that does not address the fear and anxiety of the people, creating religious illusions on the one hand and, on the other, bent on maintaining its own power and authority will eventually be rejected by them. Christianity and its theology separated from "the traditional,

Closely bound with these people's cultures, is the people's beliefs and faiths. Song observes that since the dawn of human civilization, religion in a variety of forms, from low to high, from spontaneous to institutionalized, has evolved and developed to meet people's spiritual needs. Each and every religion has its history deeply rooted in the subconscious realm of their being and existence. So, for Song it is not possible to develop and indigenous theology without penetrating and exploring these subconscious realms of the human spirit. He suggests that in order to do indigenous theology one has to immerse into indigenous popular culture and explore the roots of people's spiritual needs and longings embedded in it. Without creatively engaging in such fundamental exercise, indigenous theology continues to be merely table talks.[12] Having discussed Song's indigenous popular culture, which according to him is the foundation of a nation's culture in all aspects and layers of people's life, we can now move on to indigenous elite culture.

2.3.3. Elite Culture with Creative Imagination

Song inevitably conceives the presence of both indigenous popular culture and elite culture in every country. Elite culture according to him is a culture that consists of fine arts, music, operas, and literature. It is a culture created, appreciated and enjoyed by a relatively small number of people among the population. Having compared the elite or eyebrows culture in contrast to popular culture, Song says that popular culture is spontaneous and not manufactured. The elite culture can be identified with the process of learning to write with brush, copying from the writings of famous calligraphers repetitively until it becomes a perfect art. This is a very dry and monotonous exercise and many usually give it up halfway.[13] This is a way of imitating already existing fine arts. He says that just imitating of great calligraphers is not going to make anyone a great calligrapher.

historical and (especially) cultural ties" of the people outside the church it seeks to win for Christianity will become less and less effective and pertinent in post-Western colonial Asia or Africa. Choan-Seng Song, "From Indigenous Stories...," 113.

[12] Choan-Seng Song, "From Indigenous Stories...," 113-114.

[13] Choan-Seng Song, "From Indigenous Stories...," 114-115.

In similar vein, just imitating Western theology is not going to make anyone an indigenous theologian. Based on Jesus' phrase, "A disciple is not above the teacher…" Matthew 10:24, Song assumes that Jesus must be referring to a teacher with creative imagination, a teacher who dares to break out of the conventional rules and restrictions, challenges traditionalism, ritualism, legalism and strikes out on a different path. Likewise, Song or Jesus insists us to become unconventional theologians, daring to say as Jesus did: "You have heard that it was said to those of ancient times…but I say to you…" (Matthew 5).[14] Thus, for Song this is a key watchword to understand the context afresh. His emphasis is apparently deconstructing Western theology and the socio-cultural history written by outsiders who hardly have any indigenous cultural experience. On the other hand, he insists on to reconstruct socio-cultural history of the people based on the indigenous popular culture.

Song encourages those engaged in the creation of Taiwan's elite culture in the fields of fine arts, music, and literature because their contributions elevate Taiwan's elite culture. Many Taiwanese writers have been able to develop their own idiom and style to give expression to the struggle people of Taiwan have gone through. These powerful creativity and imagination of artistic power are not always a home-grown but they derived from many sources especially from neighbouring countries. However, their appeal, cry, passion, aspirations are all from Taiwan's indigenous popular culture. It is this indigenous popular culture that inspires them and empowers them to generate their creative imagination.[15] Song is of the view that the indigenous elite culture, to graduate from the stage of imitation, in order to become indigenously creative; it has to be nourished by nutritious substance of indigenous popular culture so that it derives inspiration from it. Nevertheless, it has to integrate external cultural elements into indigenous sources to create indigenous elite culture imbued with the indigenous spirit.[16] His emphasis on indigenous popular and elite cultures does not mean to refuse to have contacts

---

[14] Choan-Seng Song, "From Indigenous Stories…," 115.

[15] Choan-Seng Song, "From Indigenous Stories…," 116.

[16] Choan-Seng Song, "From Indigenous Stories…," 117.

with the external world. Rather, the tasks of indigenous elite culture is to make the language of indigenous popular culture intelligible to a wider human community, enabling more peoples and nations to be able to feel, to comprehend and to appreciate the sufferings and aspirations of a people and a nation. "If this is the case with indigenous culture, it is not less case with indigenous Christian theology," says Song.[17] Indigenous popular culture being a source of nutritious substance for both Christian theology and elite culture, has to nourish both of them in order to become indigenously creative and avoid any form of monotony and hegemony of Christian theology and culture.

2.3.4. Indigenous Story as Source for Indigenous Christian Theology

Song based on the indigenous popular culture and indigenous elite culture, moves on to indigenous Christian theology as its ultimate purpose. This adventure is a long but exciting undertaking, seldom attempted by Christian communities and academic theologians. According to Song, the key to understand Christian theology is story, the stories of people. Story, for him, is an excellent source for Christian theology. He views that the Christian Bible is all about stories, and this is not an accident. Jesus taught in stories, and this is not unintentional. Jesus' parables are stories, says Song;

> Story is life and life is story. There is no life without story. Stories are the core of history and history without stories is a monotonous litany, more dead than alive. Stories create community and community embodies stories. To take away stories from a community is to make an end of it. Remove stories from history, history is reduced to a mere skeleton. Lift stories from culture, all is left is an empty shell with no life in it.[18]

Song sees that Christian theology contains in most part concepts and not stories, doctrines and not living women, men and

---

[17] Choan-Seng Song, "From Indigenous Stories...," 118.

[18] Choan-Seng Song, "From Indigenous Stories...," 118.

children with countless stories of life and death, despair and hope, suffering and joy. He staunchly insists to seek indigenous stories as the primary source to develop indigenous Christian theology. He aims that stories constitute the core of indigenous popular culture and on top of that indigenous elite culture be built. Song also emphasizes the social-political stories have been part and parcel of political theology developed in Korea, Philippines and Taiwan. However, he further insists Christian theology to cross over from social-political stories to religious-cultural stories as it is inclusive of all religious stories, it means not only socio-politico-cultural stories. The earnest emphasis on religious-cultural stories does not mean less need for political theology in those countries, indeed it is needed even if the nations became free and democratic. However, according to Song, unless one finds ways to deal with indigenous religious-cultural stories, the expansion of political theology into full-fledged indigenous Christian theology will not be possible.[19] Thus, genuinely speaking, indigenous Christian theology is made possible by indigenous people's stories, a theology free from theological hegemony.

2.4. Theological Understanding of Cultures

Having discussed the inextricable relation between cultures and Christian theology, and subsequently the need for retrieving the indigenous popular culture, the task of elite culture in the context of Taiwan, and story as resource for Christian theology, Song further leads us to a theological meaning of cultures. So, we intend here to see in detail a theological meaning of culture.

2.4.1. In Search of Theological Meaning in Asian Cultures

As cited by Ya-Tang Chuang, for Song, the issue of gospel and culture is a perennial one. As a Christian theologian, born a Taiwanese in Asia, Song wrestles with the basic theological question such as "What is the relationship of our cultures with God's creation, salvation and gospel?" "How do we find the gospel of salvation in our cultures?" "What is the role of our cultures in the great plan of God's creation and salvation?" Thus, such basic queries let Song begin the

[19] Choan-Seng Song, "From Indigenous Stories...," 118.

exploration of Christian faith in the midst of cultures, religions, and histories and to construct and develop the theological meaning of Asian cultures.[20] With his new theological understanding of culture, Song begins to criticize vehemently the theological understanding of the traditional Western theology that defines culture as a belief system that differs from the Christian faith. This way of conceiving culture in a narrow sense fosters an anti-cultural mentality among Christians. He points out that this anti-culturalism commits at least two errors. First, it assumes that the Christian faith, since it is revealed, has to be free from all cultural trappings, forgetting that even the Word of God "became ***flesh*** and dwell among us." Second, "it dogmatically concludes that the images, symbols, values, worldviews and customs developed within cultures shaped by religions other than Christianity are to be rejected because they express nothing other than corruption of human mind and distortion of God's truth."[21] This anti-culturalism of the West has brought injustice to human beings as cultural beings. It has also done injustice to God, who is related to us human beings through what we are as cultural beings.[22] Song ironically asserts that Christian teaching has rejected cultures, Christian worship has alienated cultures but gospel has been basically not so.[23] Hence, keeping this in mind, a further theological exploration of what cultures really are in relation to human beings and gospel can be further discussed.

2.4.2. Culture as a Complex Whole of Human Life

Song's emphasis on culture is that, it is "a manifestation of what human beings as members of a society are and what they do. It is how they live and die, toil and labour, love and hate, hope and despair, as well as what they believe. In short, culture is human beings as individuals, as member of a family and a society, as men and women, and children related to one in a human community."[24]

[20] Ya-Tang Chuang, "Gospel and Cultures…," 2.

[21] Ya-Tang Chuang, "Gospel and Cultures…," 2.

[22] Ya-Tang Chuang, "Gospel and Cultures…," 2-3.

[23] Ya-Tang Chuang, "Gospel and Cultures…," 5-6.

[24] Ya-Tang Chuang, "Gospel and Cultures…," 6.

As already been remarked, culture for Song is not an abstract but it has history, life, born, lives and dies. What is implicit in this is that culture is human being.[25] Thus, in this respect, Song's theological approach to culture is not to deal with culture as entirely a separate entity but to deal with human beings in a particular and concrete culture. He also affirms, "we cannot treat religion and culture as a collective impersonal entity—religion without human hearts and culture without human faces."[26] This statement is in consonance with his appeal to Jesus' famous phrase "The Sabbath was made for the sake of human beings and not human beings for the Sabbath," (Mark 2:27). Sabbath, the quintessence of Jewish culture stands for a symbol of culture. The theological question that is being grappled is, it is not whether the Sabbath is good in itself, but what does it do to men and women who live in that Jewish culture. So, it is explicitly about a culture that is productive and beneficial for humankind as people live in culture. It is not that culture owns the people but it is such that the culture owes the people who own the culture, a culture that evolves out of human affairs and keeps adding with new elements as people continue to search for new meaning and fuller humanity in their religious adventures.

2.4.3. Culture and God's Creative Dynamics

Song views culture as comprehensive expression of the creative dynamic released from its origin. In the human realm, the release of creative dynamic takes forms in painting, sculpture, music, architecture, technology, and so on. The phrase 'creative dynamic' is closely related with the cultural dynamic of God's creation from which human creative power is derived. Song aptly puts it here, "Culture as a whole is none other than the manifestation of God's creative power translated into actual forms and events."[27] Thus, he understands creation with God's culture in its totality.[28] The

---

[25] Choan-Seng Song, "Freedom of Christian Theology...," 28.

[26] Ya-Tang Chuang, "Gospel and Cultures...," 6.

[27] Ya-Tang Chuang, "Gospel and Cultures...," 6.

[28] Choan-Seng Song, *Christian Mission in Reconstruction—An Asian Attempt* (Madras: Christian Literature Society, 1975), 25.

"human" dimension of culture is interrelated with the "divine" dimension because culture here implies is "human beings" and not "man-made."[29]

Song while trying to reconstruct the Christian mission in the world of plural culture, he seriously undertakes creation and incarnation as his theological basis. Reflecting on the writers of the first creation story, Song points out that the story presents a superb picture of God's power of creation becoming cultural dynamic giving forms, order and above all, life to that which is formless, chaotic and without life.[30] To him, reducing of God's creation to a "Christian" colony is a fatal mistake that Christian theology can make. In doing this, Christian theology not only rejects other religions and cultures but also rejects God who created the heavens and the earth.[31] His dealing with creation of the Bible sheds new light on the relationship between culture and religion. His view of religion in its true sense is a synthesis of culture. It is in this religion that people find the intense concentration of humankind's cultural dynamic and creative energy. "In religion the communion between the divine and the human gets expressed in visible and audible forms in an extremely heightened degree" states Song.[32] Therefore, he is of the view that it is humankind's religious genius that gives birth to culture. In other words, the source and origin of humankind's cultural dynamic is to be found in humankind's communion with dynamic of God that is being embodied in His creation.[33] Thus, Song advocates that Christian must speak of the cultural task of Christian mission that should make an effort to search for and appreciate different shapes in which cultural dynamic of God's creation takes in different cultural and historical contexts. There is, for him, no dichotomy of Christian and non-Christian cultures. He states that "Christian mission must therefore be first of all a critique of culture. If the word critique sounds a little too judgmental in connotation, we may call it theology

[29] Ya-Tang Chuang, "Gospel and Cultures…," 7.

[30] Choan-Seng Song, *Christian Mission,* 25.

[31] Ya-Tang Chuang, "Gospel and Cultures…," 8.

[32] Choan-Seng Song, *Christian Mission,* 26.

[33] Choan-Seng Song, *Christian Mission,* 26.

of cultures. It is a theological perception and interpretation of the spirituality of a particular culture in the light of the biblical faith in God as the creator."[34] Based on this understanding of creation, he re-orients the understanding of gospel and cultures.

2.4.4. Gospel Incarnates in Cultures

The incarnational theology of the New Testament describes how gospel incarnates in cultures. "The Word became flesh and lived among us," (John 1:14). Flesh here refers not only to the historical Jesus, but the "historical Christ." The Word has taken human form not only in Judeo-Christian culture but also in Asian cultures.[35] Also for Song, incarnation fundamentally does not mean God dealing with demons and angels but with human beings. "It means Jesus was a full-fledged human being. It also means salvation in the Christian sense is not unrelated to the salvation human beings seek and long for in their respective cultures."[36] With this basic understanding of the Word taking human form, Song is led to a more explicit of the Word-culture relation in Asian context.

Song embarks on incarnational theology from the perspective of God's mission of enfleshment[37] in his well-articulated work on *Christian Mission in Reconstruction.*[38] From the point of mission of enfleshment, he views that the task of Christian mission is not to Christianize the world but to make contribution to the renewal of civilizations deeply rooted in other religions. Although, it sounds shocking yet it is not a betrayal of Christian faith. He reiterates "the chief task of Christian mission is to let the faith in Jesus Christ become

---

[34] Choan-Seng Song, *Christian Mission,* 28.

[35] Ya-Tang Chuang, "Gospel and Cultures…," 9.

[36] Choan-Seng Song, "Freedom of Christian Theology…," 32.

[37] Enfleshment: Song states that God's mission of enfleshment in Jesus Christ is God becoming what he is not. This entails the risk of God losing His own identity. It is paradoxical to say that God is becoming no longer God. However for Song, this miracle of enfleshment does not result in God forfeiting His identity as Creator and Redeemer. On the contrary, Song says, "By becoming other than what He is, namely, by becoming present and manifest in Jesus Christ, He has revealed Himself as what He truly is. This is the heart of the paradox of Christian faith."

[38] Choan-Seng Song, *Christian Mission,* 55.

the germinal element which enables civilization to be renewed as witness to the glory of God's creation and manifestation of the presence of God as Saviour in the world."[39] Owing to this concept of incarnational mission, Song does not necessitate converting people into the fold of Christian community and integrating them into the religious structure of the church.[40] Song stands for Christ-centered mission over church-centered mission. Christ centered mission for Song means, Jesus Christ is at the intersection of the divine dimension and the human dimension at every stage of history from creation to incarnation. Therefore, in Jesus Christ, God saturates the whole history of human beings and the world.[41] According to him, Christ-centered mission defines the nature and function of the church and therefore, the church is an event rather than an organization, fellowship rather than church order.[42] The incarnation brings both judgmental and forgiveness to the world so the gospel that incarnated in cultures does not compromise with cultures but brings judgment and forgiveness, death and resurrection to the cultures.[43] God's love is the essence of the incarnation in accordance with the New Testament teaching of God's agape-love in its fullness. Implicit in the incarnation is "becoming" and "changing." Due to this agape-love, God is acted upon and moved by human beings who have become prisoners of their own sin. It also shows how God is capable of change for the sake of human salvation. In other words, the incarnation reflects on the "changeability"[44] of the gospel.[45] Because of this risk God has taken that we are saved, and the world has hope and future. Since incarnation of God is the God of incarnation, an alternative term for this is equated with the

[39] Choan-Seng Song, *Christian Mission,* 57.

[40] Choan-Seng Song, *Christian Mission,* 55.

[41] Choan-Seng Song, *Christian Mission,* 61.

[42] Choan-Seng Song, *Christian Mission,* 63.

[43] Ya-Tang Chuang, "Gospel and Cultures...," 9.

[44] Changeability of the Gospel: the heart of the gospel is that God becomes flesh in humanity, incarnates in Jesus Christ and through him in us all. How bold God is to change himself into human form. God risks becoming less than God and risks tasting the agony of God-forsakenness in Jesus on the cross.

[45] Ya-Tang Chuang, "Gospel and Cultures...," 10.

God of transposition. God transposes God-self freely in the world that has been created by God. God's transposition simply denotes the transposition of the gospel. "When transposed from its biblical world to other cultural worlds, the gospel undergoes change itself as well as causing these other worlds to change," quoted Ya-Tang Chuang.[46] Furthermore, Song puts it very convincingly that culture as being originated and incarnated by God's creative dynamics; it has the power for self-purging, self-cleaning and self-criticism.[47] Thus this 'changeability,' God becoming what he is not, is implicit in the incarnational theology. Therefore, `Incarnation' simply implies the nature of change and transposition, so does the gospel undergo change merely because it envisions to appropriate the power of self-purging, self-cleaning and self-criticism within a cultural milieu for the transformation of the whole world.

2.4.5. Theological Semantics of Culture

Having argued how the gospel incarnated in cultures, Song stands against Christians to negate and conquer cultures, but to train our Christian theological minds to perceive God's judgment and salvation working through men, women and children in their own cultures. Cultures are deemed friends to the gospel. Gospel and culture reciprocates one another, in a sense, gospel illuminates culture and culture also illuminates our understanding of the Gospel.[48] Cultures, thus gives us new "theological horizons," and gives a new understanding of God, the Creator and Saviour of all nations and peoples. For Song, this new understanding of cultures gives him a "new theological horizons," to explore this, Song describe three levels of culture. According to him, each language has its grammar of culture, syntax of culture and semantics of culture. Although, they are considered three different things but they are correlative. First, the grammar of culture:[49] Each culture, just like each language, has its

[46] Ya-Tang Chuang, "Gospel and Cultures...," 10.

[47] Ya-Tang Chuang, "Gospel and Cultures...," 11.

[48] Ya-Tang Chuang, "Gospel and Cultures...," 12.

[49] Grammar of culture: it refers to the rules about the use of the elements or components such as knowledge, belief, art, morals, laws and custom. It is a science

own grammar different from the grammar of other cultures. Having failed to understand or neglecting of the grammar of a culture, one has misunderstood at first step.

Second, is syntax of culture,[50] it tells that it is the sentence structure, and not the individual words, that is the basic meaning. Song, having applied syntax of culture, he advocates the mutual relationships and constituting structure of those elements and components of culture. According to Song, "culture consists of "sentences" which are made of elements such as customs, arts, morals, and beliefs. All such "sentences" disclose different aspects of the complex whole called culture. If one judges culture because of its flaws without considering its complicated relationships, one commits the fallacy of *pars pro toto.*"[51] Here, Song advocates the need to study the grammar and syntax of one's culture to let that grammar and syntax interact with the grammar and syntax of the gospel. This study prevents the reader from misunderstanding and at the same time leads one deep into the semantic level of culture.

Third, semantics of culture,[52] in the case of a cultural complex that includes religious beliefs, semantics becomes the heart of the theological inquiry.[53] Song further states, "At the centre of theological semantics of culture are human persons in their relations to God. Human persons create the space for meaning and then destroy it; we fill time with meaning and nullify it. Meaning of culture, then, has to be personal and not impersonal, relational and not private, historical and not fictional, that is, meaning affects human beings in their relations to the world in which they live and, of course, in their relations to God."[54] Exploring the semantics of culture, those

---

of basic rules of how these basic components are used and expressed in the proper way prescribed by that cultural complex whole.

[50] Syntax of culture: in language, syntax is the arrangement of word forms to show their mutual relations in the essence.

[51] Ya-Tang Chuang, "Gospel and Cultures…," 12.

[52] Semantics of culture: in linguistic, semantics is a study of meaning. It is a discipline that pursues the significance of things. It is an art that penetrates the inner depths of beings.

[53] Ya-Tang Chuang, "Gospel and Cultures…," 13.

[54] Ya-Tang Chuang, "Gospel and Cultures…," 13.

unrelated to Christianity in its origin and history, help us to deepen our understanding of God's creating and redeeming activity outside the Christian cultures.

2.4.6. The Culture of God's Reign[55]

Song prefers the 'reign of God' to the 'kingdom of God' with a view to avoid the earthly kingdom type. For Song, the Greek phrase *basileia tou theou* or the kingdom of God does not correctly express Jesus' message of God's reign. It misrepresents it as it conveys the notions of national territory, feudal system, and monarchical structure, in a word, a `culture of authoritarianism.' On the other hand, the expression the reign of God although is not totally adequate, it at least does not represent the notion of a boundary, be it political or religious. It reflects God who exercises the rule and not the ecclesiastical authorities.[56] Thus, it is opposed to earthly monarchy.[57] Song, in the light of this God's reign, sees humans in cultures so much exploited and corrupted by the drive for power and property especially an autocratic government, a corrupt regime, an exploited economic system, transnational corporations. They are not instituted by God, the Creator, and not desired by God, the Saviour. The plights are made by human beings.[58] Song points out the negative and dark sides of culture especially with that of Asia, what he calls as a culture of authoritarianism and suppression that has prevailed for centuries and is still ruling today. He states, "What we have in many countries in Asia is a culture of suffering within a culture of domination."[59] To live in such culture of domination and authoritarianism tend to

---

[55] God's reign: according to Song, the reign of God is not a religious competing for influence with other religions; it is not the victory of justice over injustice in human community. It is not an emancipation of the soul from the shackles of this world. Rather it is the power that empowers us to live in the midst of adversities and despairs. It is neither a spatial nor a static concept but it is a dynamic concept, an action term that must be charges with energy, power and vitality. C.S. Song, *Jesus and the Reign of God* (Minneapolis: Fortress Press, 1993), 154.

[56] C.S. Song, *Jesus and the Reign,* 39.

[57] C.S. Song, *Jesus and the Reign,* 154.

[58] C.S. Song, *Jesus and the Reign,* 90-91.

[59] Ya-Tang Chuang, "Gospel and Cultures...," 14.

foster self-abasement, deception and corruption. Having exposed culture of domination and oppression in the light of God's reign, Song further leads us to culture of empowerment.

2.4.7. Culture of Empowerment

To start with the culture of empowerment, Song begins with Jesus' declaration that the reign of God belongs to the poor and oppressed. Despite the staunch claim for the reign of God in the context of poor and oppressed, Song indicates in a way how they are still downtrodden, not only socially but also religiously. Although, the good news of God's reign assures especially to oppressed and the poor yet they are still downtrodden not only socially but religiously, it does not bring any change in the lives of the poor and oppressed. Over to this problem, Song laments, "With neither institution nor structure to back them how could they work toward the realization of God's reign?"[60] For him, it is such that the people are unaware about the reign of God because they have to realize that the people "themselves are potentially the reign of God, that is, God has given them the potentialities—the power—to be the reign of God. To make them conscious of that power, to help them realize that in talking about the reign of God he is talking about them and not about religious concept, to enable them to take steps to change their life and their community—this must be what Jesus has to do."[61] A culture of empowerment is what Jesus sets out to build with the people—a culture without which the reign of God would remain a mere concept and a pious illusion unrelated to people's everyday life of hardships, fear and anxiety.[62] The reign of God creates a culture of empowerment. It is a culture of empowerment. Jesus, who heals the sick, comforts those in sorrow, protects women and men maltreated by the rich and the powerful, is the reign of God. And together with these people he has created a culture of empowerment over against the culture of intimation and exploitation.[63] Thus, the reign of God

[60] C.S. Song, *Jesus and the Reign*, 91.

[61] C.S. Song, *Jesus and the Reign*, 91.

[62] C.S. Song, *Jesus and the Reign*, 130.

[63] C.S. Song, *Jesus and the Reign* 136.

empowers people, the poor and the oppressed to strive for justice, and their human rights. It also empowers them to get organized to change their status quo.

2.4.8. Culture of Protest

Within the culture of empowerment is culture of protest, which takes action against the oppressive and dehumanized structures for radical change. Song points out those especially institutionalized religions[64] which have often proved an obstacle for change. Song identifies the negative side of religion in which he necessitates a "religion itself needs to change for the world to be able to change. And a change called for in a religion must be a radical change, a change with profound theological implications for our relations with God and other people. This in essence is the heart of the prophetic movement in ancient Israel."[65] Song brings out a suitable example in and through the life of prophet Amos who spoke against the rich and the powerful in soul-stirring words when the theocratic system of society and government did not guarantee freedom and equality for the people. Such a disposition pictured is "a culture of protest—a culture in which God and the poor meet, a culture that grows out of social oppression and economic injustice."[66] The *reign of God is a culture of protest.*[67] Jesus' reign of God is a culture of protest when Jesus declared, "Blessed are you who are in need, the reign of God is yours" (Luke 6:20b). Song calls this a bombshell.

---

[64] "...The Hindu doctrine of karma, for example, promising reincarnation into a higher caste as a reward for diligently fulfilling the obligations of one's station in his life, certainly discouraged social and political protest. Protestant Pentecostal sects in the United States, Latin America, and Africa downgrade deprivation here on earth and, by concentrating on communion with the Holy Spirit and the rewards of heaven, which are vouchsafed the faithful, help, reconcile their members to a lowly social and economic status. Similarly doctrines encouraging either meek acceptance of suffering or withdrawal from the tribulations of human society can be found in other religions." C.S. Song, *Jesus and the Reign,* 95.

[65] C.S. Song, *Jesus and the Reign,* 96.

[66] C.S. Song, *Jesus and the Reign,* 96.

[67] C.S. Song, *Jesus and the Reign,* 96.

> They are not quiet stars but flashes of lightening followed by a thunder of surprise and amazement. Jesus' reign of God is not a moral exhortation; it is an indictment against society. It is not a wise counsel for political reform; it is a strong protest against the politics of the naked power. It is not a spiritual advice for change in a religion; it turns upside down the time-honoured traditions of faith and practice.[68]

2.5. Evaluation of Song's Theology of Cultures

Despite having dealt comprehensively on Song's theology of cultures in the context of Asia, however, except for women's subjugation, there are certain detrimental cultures to which Song is subtle of those. With regard to the women's issue of subjugation, Song says, "Appeal to the Bible for the supremacy of a male God does not relieve the suffering of the women in Asia caused by the church with its patriarchal structure and its unsound theology."[69] Some common oppressive and inhuman cultures can be reckoned here such as issues related to capitalistic culture that promotes private ownership of the means of production, creation of goods or services for profit, accumulation of capital, competitive market and wage labor.[70] Individualistic culture obviously is losing the ties between individuals in the society as everyone is expected to look after him/herself and his/her immediate family.[71] Dalit and tribal cultures are another two important cultures which cannot go unnoticed. Despite

---

[68] C.S. Song, *Jesus and the Reign*, 97.

[69] C.S. Song, *Tell Us Our Names*, 44-45.

[70] "Capitalism" is an economic system that became dominant in the Western world following the demise of feudalism. There is general agreement that elements of capitalism include private ownership of the means of production, creation of goods or services for profit the accumulation of capital, competitive market and wage labour. http://en.wikipedia.org/wiki/Capitalism, 12:53, 09.12.2011.

[71] "Individualism," opposite of this is collectivism that is the degree to which individuals are integrated into groups. On the individualistic side we find societies in which the ties between individuals are loose: everyone is expected to look after him/herself and his/her immediate family. in http://www.clearlycultural.com/geert-hofstede-cultural-dimensions/individualism/, 1.02, 09.12.2011

the Dalits being hardworking people, yet the culture in which they live now is within the dominant caste Hindu (DCHs) set by the Brahmins, which is also called parasitic culture in which the DCHs have built up so much dependency on the Dalits for their basics needs particularly the Brahmins and Kshatriyas.[72] The process of globalization has largely affected the lives of the tribal. Cultural universalism is introduced. The tribal such as Dongria tribe, Jarawa tribe, Chengara, Plachimada, Adivasi, Narmada tribes etc. who have mainly confined to hills and forests, have now sought their abortion into the regional and national mainstream. In many ways globalization destroys tribal identities. In such a case, globalization is seen as a multi-pronged attack on the very foundation of the tribal existence besides the issue of marginalization of their indigenous culture.[73] Another prevalent culture is consumerist/tic culture, it is used to describe the tendency of the people to identify strongly with products or services they consume, especially those with commercial brand names and perceived appeal, e.g. a luxury car, designed clothing, or expensive jewelry. A culture which is permeated by consumerism can be considered as a consumer culture or a market culture[74] and Cyber culture[75] are not dealt sufficiently if not overlooked in Song's theology of cultures.

Although, Song has not dealt specifically many prevailing unhealthy cultures, yet it is conspicuous that he left no stone

---

[72] "Dalit Culture," in http://www.ambedkar.org/ssc/indiansociety/dcult.htm, 01:11, 9.12.2011.

[73] Developmental strategies under the New Economic Policies led to a process of conscious and systematic annihilation of culture and identity of the first people-the Adivasis-of this country. This process of globalization has invaded India since the introduction of New Liberalization Policy. The socio-cultural change among the tribal communities has no doubt empowered the tribals; however, their cultural identity is under severe stress._http://www.lscac.msu.ac.th/book/149.pdf, 6:45 pm, 17.01. 2012.

[74] "Consumerism," in http://en.wikipedia.org/wiki/Consumerism 10:55, 09.12.2011.

[75] Christine Quinlan, "The Harmful Effects of Cyber Culture on Youth," (University of Ontario Institute of Technology). Criminal activities such as File Sharing, Gaming, Chat Rooms and Cybersex are prevalent. *https://ir.library.dc-uoit.ca/bitstream/10155/52/1/QUINLAN.doc, Jan.19th, 2012.*

unturned for every miniscule of oppression that exists in the society in any respect that is reflected in the *culture of protest*. Song indeed is critical of the dehumanized and inhumane elements involved in the prevailing cultures of every nation, community, tribe etc. Therefore, with this regard, he strongly advocates the culture of empowerment and the culture of protest.

2.6. Conclusion

Having dealt with what Song's theology of cultures aspires and aims for, some few significant and noteworthy can be underscored in the conclusion. Song seeing Asian context with multi-religious and cultural diversities, he has made an attempt to penetrate into Asian world taking into consideration the cultures of different peoples and nations without demeaning and devaluing any of a particular culture. He is against Christian culture as a norm by which other cultures have to be judged. Every culture is equally significant and theologically redemptive, there is neither superior nor inferior culture, or normative or non-normative by which other cultures are to be judged over others. Song coherently puts it in a way God is active in every culture, "God's salvation can no longer be explained in terms of a history moving forward along a straight line. To explain God's salvation in this way is to explain it away. God moves in all directions: God moves forward, no doubt, but also sideways and even backwards."[76] This simply explicates to us that God works in every culture, the distinction between culture of Christianity and other cultures is overcome because God's redeeming love has no boundary albeit demarcation of Christian and non-Christian culture is assumed usually by traditional Christian theology. God's redeeming activity is beyond human comprehension. Thereby, denunciation of any culture could be illogic and even be sinful.

Song, by dealing cultures from different perspectives, he does not cease with mere understanding of what cultures are in relation to theology or Christianity. Rather, he goes further by taking seriously into consideration what cultures are embodying in them. Therefore, he undertakes seriously about the elements and components of the

[76] C.S. Song, *Tell Us Our Names*, 16.

cultures such as stories, folktales, folksongs, folklores, legends, myths etc. together Song identifies them as Story theology in which Song has given major treatment within his discussion on Asian resources. Hence, story theology as part of Asian resources, will be continual efforts in our discussion on Asian resources in the succeeding chapters.

Chapter 3

Theologizing Asian Resources: Story Theology

3.1. Introduction

For Song, Culture is never an abstract idea. Rather, culture has a history; it is historical. Culture has a life; it is born, lives and dies. Outside the life and history of a people and nation, there is no culture. While dealing with Asian cultures, Song accentuates that within cultures are embodied stories, folklores, folktales, history, religions, images and symbols which of these are intrinsically related with cultures. Indeed, these are the constituent parts of cultures which are to be uncovered in light of Song's theology of cultures. The constituent parts of cultures as an Asian resources are, Song's points of departure for doing Christian theology.

3.2 Doing Theology with Asian Resources

Before getting into the discussion on story theology, it is worth explicating its resources from which story theology has its cradle. Song being aware of Asian resources with its diverse natures such as folk tales, histories, religions, symbols and images, he prerequisites these resources if Asian theology to be viable and distinctive from its western garb.

3.2.1. Theology with Asian Folk Literature

Song opines that with the introduction of theology with Asian folk literature, many are puzzled, confused and shocked those spellbound by time-honoured theological concepts and norms of Western theology. With the assumption that these are pagan stories and the church has nothing to do with them. Most Christian theologies done are of lofty subject-matter with a pre-concept that the task of Christian theology is to think "deep thing" of God and about God. "Nothing less than abstruse language, words and concepts worthy of the reality that transcends human apprehension, systems and structure capable of logically disclosing the divine mystery, are considered to be theological," states Song[1] Doing theology with concepts and metaphysics among the theological experts do not reflect the sweat and labour, hopes and despairs, sighs and longings of men, women and children who are struggling for survival against the forces of nature and human society that threaten their existence and deprive them of the meaning of life.[2]

Song, thus, advocates the importance of re-discovery of folktales, the fact that the Christian Bible is basically a story book, that it is a book consisting largely of people's stories and folktales. He observes, "These are very human stories, stories of love and hate, stories of lust and greed, stories of treachery and conflicts, and also stories of how God's redeeming love shines out of the ruins of human life and history."[3] Thus, the same stories that the Bible contains about are found in the living societies and communities in Asia. Reclaiming them is reclaiming Asian humanity, immersing in them will lead Asians to touch the roots of their Asian being. The surprising thing about the fact of stories of Asian is that the echoes

---

[1] Choan Seng (C.S.), "Christian Theology—An Asian Way," in *Doing Theology with Asian Resources: Theology and Cultures*, 2 (1995): 25.

[2] Choan Seng (C.S.), "Christian Theology...," 26.

[3] Choan Seng (C.S.), "Christian Theology...," 26.

of the humanity seeking liberation are heard, which are contained in the stories of the Bible.[4] One example is recalled in which Song gives an illustration of folktales as a source for story theology. This folktale is called "The Mirror" a Chinese origin as early as the T'ang dynasty (A.D. 618-906).

> Wang the Third was a stupid man. One day his wife wanted him to buy her a wooden comb, and, being afraid that he would forget it, she pointed at the narrow moon crescent in the sky and said, "Buy me a wooden comb, but it must be like the moon in the sky."
>
> A few days later, the moon shone full and round in the sky. Wang the Third remembered what his wife had told him, and, since his purchase was to be as round as the moon, he bought a round mirror and took it home.
>
> The moment his wife saw it, she stamped on the ground, fled back to her parents' house, and said to her mother, "My husband has taken a concubine." The Mother-in-law looked into the mirror and said with a sigh, "If only he had chosen a young woman! Why did he take such a hideous old hag?"
>
> Later they brought the case before the district judge. When he saw the mirror, he said, "How dare you people, when you have a quarrel, dress up just like me! It's unbelievable!"[5]

The locus of this folktale, says Song, is the reflections in the mirror. The story of Mirror tells us that the wife, the mother-in-law, and the judge fail to recognize the reflection of their true images. When they see their reflections in the mirror, they express negative images on their own reflections. They do not like their own self-image. Song says this tale can be "a parable for Chinese theology" also in our case of Asian theology. Although, a mirror called theology has been given to us yet Asian theologians or Christians tend to take

---

[4] Choan Seng (C.S.), "Christian Theology…," 26.

[5] C.S. Song, *Tell Us Our Names*, 3.

a negative view toward the image reflected in the theological mirror and tend to be upset by it, thinking the image of the mirror is the adulteration of the true image that God has given us.[6] Kyounghee Shin observes that Song focuses on two major possibilities of using the folk-tale as a theological resource. One is the possibility of self-exploration and self-discovery for Asian theologians and Asian Christians; the second is the support for Asian ways of knowing as the core of method of Asian story theology.[7]

3.2.2. Theology with History as People's Movement

A Christian theology to be crucial and genuine, Song gives serious attention to 'history of the insignificant' or unrecognized. His view is that God does not deal with the history in general but in specific ways. It is a specific people that evoke God's passionate concern and involvement. Therefore, the main concern in this aspect is not an official history, the history written by the victors and conquerors, fabricated by those who by force usurped from God and people the power to rule or manufactured by dictators and oppressors to glorify their greatness at the expense of the countless men, women and children without power to defend themselves from exploitation and tyranny. Rather, this kind of text-book history, says Song, "must be unmasked, it lies exposed and harm it has done to people must be removed."[8] However, what is more important is, getting at history as stories of nameless people, or not recorded in the history books but without whom history would be just an account of human insanity and a testimony to God's impotence. Thus, Song utters, "To regain our faith in God as the Lord of history we must first see ourselves how our people rise from the ashes of destruction and death from one generation to the next, how we who are living are part of the vision and dream of

---

[6] C.S. Song, *Tell Us Our Names,* 4.

[7] Kyounghee Shin, "Theological Truth of Folk-Tales and Christian Education through an Analysis of Song's Story Theology," in old.religiouseducation.net/proceedings/Shin_Theological...13-12-2011.

[8] Choan Seng (C.S.), "Christian Theology...," 27.

the people who have gone before us."[9] It is unimaginable for Song an Asian history less related to the God of the Christian Bible, especially people outside officially documented history, who are insignificant, deprived and oppressed.

3.2.3. Theology with Asian Religions

Asia being the home of world religions such as Buddhism, Hinduism, Islam, Confucianism and Taoism, flourished with primal beliefs and rites, including Shamanism. Song comments that "In the years after World War II these religions have not only undergone resurgence but variations of them in the form of new religions have mushroomed like bamboo shoots after rain to fill the spiritual void left by the devastating war and to respond to the futile sense of life created by increasingly profit-oriented competitive society."[10] The main concern in this aspect is to explore how religious faith affects the life of the believers, played a part in the tradition and ethos of a society, and becomes related to the oppressive ideological and political forces. It is not to deal with the official history of religions but in the stories of religious faith and institutions lived and experienced by ordinary believers. It is a desire to understand what is going on in their mind as they offer incense at the temple, with hearts filled with despair and hope. It is also an attempt to grasp a sense of liberation a Shamanistic priestess experiences in a male-dominated family and society as she is engaged in ecstasy in her religious duties. Thus, it is an attempt to touch theologically the souls that seek to emancipate from the bondage of life behind convents and monasteries. Men and women with courage and commitment to their faith, rise in revolt against feudal and dictatorial rulers at a great cost of their lives.[11] There is a mysterious dynamism behind each religious practice that helps them to satiate their desire for life and liberation in accordance with their belief. This mystery that emancipates from the bondage of life needs to be touched theologically.

---

[9] Choan Seng (C.S.), "Christian Theology…," 27.

[10] Choan Seng (C.S.), "Christian Theology…," 27.

[11] Choan Seng (C.S.), "Christian Theology…," 27-28.

3.2.4. Theology with Symbols and Images

Song states,

> We human being are makers of symbols and images that give expression to who we are, how we are related to one another, to the world, to nature, and of course, to God. When it comes to such symbol-image making, we Asians have proved to be more prolific than other people... Symbols and images are at their most explicit in religious faith. But we also know that powerful symbols and images are at the very heart of social changes and upheavals.[12]

According to Song, in symbols and images the dichotomy of the sacred and profane, the religious and the secular, is abolished. Penetrating them at their deepest source will make us realize that there is no question of what is Christian and not Christian. Thus, Song says, "Through exploration of symbols and images, from religious ones that have held a religious community together to the ones that serve to bring about revolutionary change in society, we may encounter a theological world in which God and humanity are engaged in struggle for human liberation both here and now and in the future to come."[13] For instance, religious images and cultural symbols, abundant in the life of people in Yogyakarta, have not lost their innocence entirely. Song perceives in them a genuine longing of men and women for justice, love and peace amidst the rough and tumble of this world.[14] Related to this, Song cites a statue of Buddha at the Borobudur Temple in the central Java, Indonesia with a massive construction dating from the 8th century and enduring symbol of human longing for land of Nirvana. There the symbol of symbols, image of images was the only statue of the Buddha left open to full view:

> Seated cross-legged in lotus fashion, the eye lightly closed and the lips gently pressed, facing the pilgrims and tourists

---

[12] Choan Seng (C.S.), "Christian Theology...,," 29.

[13] Choan Seng (C.S.), "Christian Theology...,," 29.

[14] Choan Seng (C.S.), "Christian Theology...," 29.

> from far and near, from Indonesia and from overseas, who climb the hill towards him, for more than one thousand years. How much woe and joy, how much despair and hope of these fellow human beings of his he has absorbed into his body, soul and mind! His closed lips have uttered words of comfort and hope to many a perplexed soul. His whole frame, though maintaining supreme serenity, has contained the suffering and pain of those women and men who come to him for rescue from the miseries of life and for liberation from the tyranny of death.[15]

Through these found symbols and images of Buddha statue, Song finds it a clue to doing theology with symbols and images in Asia. It is a way to realize God disclosing more than one way what is in God's mind. Similar to this is Jesus' break out of the boundaries set by his own religious tradition from time to time, and grasp the meaning of what Jesus is reported to have said to Nicodemus, a Jewish rabbi: "The wind (or the spirit) blows where it wills' (John 3:8). To let this Spirit take us where it wills in Asia is the beginning of *theo*-logical wisdom."[16] It was not confined by the time-honoured Judaism, or by Christian churches today but the Spirit reveals to whomever He wants, this is where Asian Christian theology be crucial about it as we engage with cultures theologically.

3.3. Story Theology

Story theology or theology of story is one of the most pivotal in Song's theology of cultures. Ya-Tang Chuang has delineated that although Song's theology is understood in varied names and titles such as theology of cultures, theology of transposition, third-eye theology, cultural theology, however, Song prefers the description of story theology as an appropriate means to qualify his theological world. Story theology is most fundamental and prominent in Song's theological work.[17] It is rightly observed that Song's theology of

[15] Choan Seng (C.S.), "Christian Theology...," 29.

[16] Choan Seng (C.S.), "Christian Theology...,," 29-30.

[17] Ya-Tang Chuang, "Practicing Contextual Theology in Contemporary Taiwan: An Enquiry into the Theological Method of Selected Contextual

cultures is crammed with folktales, folksongs, legends, stories etc., thus, story theology can be said to have its central place in the theology of cultures.

3.3.1. Theological-Biblical Basis of Story Theology and Its Significance

The phrase "Theological-Biblical" is to simply indicate that Song has the stories of the Bible as its theological basis and the living stories of Asians on the other hand, stories outside the Bible. Hence, we aptly look at how story is related to dream, vision and its significance within a theological milieu.

3.3.1.1. Story is Dream and Dream is Story

Song states, "Story is conceived in the womb of dreams, nurtured and developed in it. And when the womb cannot hold it any longer, it gives birth to it. As a baby arrives from the womb of its mother, a story, when it matures, is discharged from the womb of dreams to be told in the circles of children, men and women. If it is a good, story, it will be told from one generation to another generation, good in the sense of compelling."[18] Joseph's dream is one such an appropriate example, which Song has brought out here. He says, future is won by those who dare to dream and to tell their dreams in stories. Joseph has dreamed extraordinary dreams and not being able to keep them to himself, he tells them to his brothers. To cut short the dream, despite all the harsh treatment from his brothers and rebuke from his parents, at last Joseph's dream came true by becoming the most influential politician in Egypt only second to Pharaoh. Thus, he stresses that story is dream and dream is story. He, citing the Australian phrase, "Story time is dream time or vice versa." Future belongs to those who dare to dream and strive to convert their dream to stories, stories of struggle, and stories of suffering, also stories of hope, faith and compassion. He also further stresses that all

---

Theologians of Taiwan," in *JTCA The Journal of Theologies and Cultures in Asia*, Vol. 6 (2007), 147.

[18] C.S. Song, "In the Beginning were Stories, not Texts," in *Theologies and Cultures: Contextual Theologies in Taiwan*, 5/1 (June 2008), 5.

prophets of ancient Israel and Judah were dreamers, such as Isaiah, Jeremiah, Ezekiel etc. at the critical juncture of their nation's history, they dreamed powerful dreams, fantastic dreams, out of the world dreams, then proceeded to tell their people stories of their dreams.[19] Asian communities are full of stories that are significant, especially at bedtimes—stories are told and retold by their parents to lullaby the children. Sometimes parents narrate different folktales at bonfire place to entertain the children and sometimes at the hearth before the children go to sleep. Every child loves listening to those stories but without understanding what they really mean.

3.3.1.2. In the Beginning were Stories

Song's source of story theology also has its origin from the Bible. Creation stories of Genesis 1:1-2, stresses Song that in the beginning were stories. Life begins with story; the whole universe begins with story. Creation does not begin with a horrendous explosion called big-bang, but with an idyllic story of how God created it, "in the beginning when God created the heavens and the earth."[20] This is the story of creation handed down by our ancestors from one generation to the next. Although, his conviction rests upon the unscientific account of how the universe came into being, yet Song denies an illusionary tale of an irrational mind. His conviction is that creation is God's story of Him taking the charge of the vast universe, big-bang or no big-bang. The significance of which he could say is that, "It is an old story, as old as the beginning of creation itself, but it becomes when it is told in different versions in an indefinite variety of ways. When human beings are faced with turbulence in the voyage of life, confronted with the world in chaos, encountered tragedy in history, they return to the beginning for God's assurance."[21] Here Song is reflecting on the prophets addressing the captives to listen to their words of God. In such a situation the prophets invited his audience, though old, ancient and out-dated, "to listen again and again until it was transformed

---

[19] C.S. Song, "In the Beginning...," 6.

[20] C.S. Song, "In the Beginning...," 10.

[21] C.S. Song, "In the Beginning...," 10.

into a new story, until it became their own story, a story of hope and faith, a story of a new beginning of their life and history."[22] This is how the story plays a vital role in the life of the people especially in the lowest ebb of their lives that inspires and gives hope in their hopelessness.

3.3.1.3. Life is the Heart of Story

For Song life is the main concern of the Story-God. The creation story in the Hebrew Bible is the story of life, life of universe, life of all things in the sky and on the earth, the life beyond the time-space frame of our existence. "Let the earth bring forth living creatures of every kind" (Gen. 124), and "Let us make humankind in our image, according to our likeness," (Gen.1:26) and in another creation story account, it says "God formed human beings from the dust of the ground and breathed into their nostril the breath of life and they became living beings."[23] What we are interested in these is, "life." It is God's interest in the life of human beings that God's stories are formed, created, told and retold. On the one hand, Song goes on to say that "life is the perennial concern of humanity and it is around life that stories are told and retold—origin of life, passages of life, and immortality of life."[24] Song's view is that both God and human beings are concerned with life, and this concern of life is reflected in stories.

3.3.1.4. Inherent Relationships between Story and Theology

Song, in a way he overcomes gospel and culture dichotomy, views that story and theology as two sides of the same coin, which is inseparable. Thus, he states,

> Story and theology are inseparable. Where there is story, there is theology. A story worthy of its name is a story that grips you in the depths of your hearts and minds, forces you to look deeply into yourself and into human nature, and compels you to examine relations between you and

[22] C.S. Song, "In the Beginning...," 10-11.

[23] C.S. Song, "In the Beginning...," 17.

[24] C.S. Song, "In the Beginning...," 18.

> other human beings, between human beings and God. If this is what story does, it is already profoundly theological. It invites us to reflect in the roots of who we are and what the world around us is, and ultimately who and what God must be. Story is the matrix of theology.[25]

Separating theology from story can be but only to its detriment for Song says, "If in the beginning was the story, if that story becomes translated into the story for generations of Christians, into the history of the world and the lives of you and me, and most important of all, if God loves stories, it is inconceivable for theology to be theology when it keeps aloof from stories, and even worse, when it detaches itself from stories."[26] Thus, for him theology to be theology, it must be story theology. It could be equivalent to say that theology without story is a theology that deals God only in conceptual and metaphysical terms. He further stresses the internal and inherent relationships between story and theology in that he affirms story as containing within itself seeds of theology, and the theological task is to identify theological seeds in stories, investigate the environments in which they grow, inquire ways in which they impact people and their surroundings as they grow. However, the effort of theology, says Song, "does not stop here. It will develop, and draw implications from what they have perceived in stories and from ways in which stories are created and recreated, told and retold, in different settings and conditions, by different people in their different life situations."[27] Song is here concerned of the stories outside Christianity which have potentially contained theological seeds because stories outside Christianity are more numerous than stories in Christianity. These stories, says Song, are equally rich in theological meanings because they are stories of how people struggle for faith, hope and love in the midst of fear, pain and suffering. He further asserts that if they are stories of faith, hope and love then it can equally be legitimate source for Christian theology. Such as Buddhist stories, Hindu, Muslim, Jewish, Confucian or stories of

[25] C.S. Song, "Story is the Matrix...," 28.

[26] C.S. Song, "Story is the Matrix...," 29.

[27] C.S. Song, "Story is the Matrix...," 29.

primal religions. These stories of different religions, in light of the beginning story as the story of God, can be Christian stories.[28]

3.3.1.5. In Story Theology, Gospel and Cultures-Dichotomy is overcome

Closely related with story and theology is, gospel and cultures. Ya-Tang Chuang has pointed out that although Song followed Coe's direction of contextualization, he develops doubt about the theological efforts of "indigenization," "acculturation" and "inculturation."[29] Song questionably puts a statement, "All these efforts, however laudable, presuppose that the culture that represents Christianity is the norm by which other cultures are to be evaluated and changed. Implicit in this approach is the transformation model—the gospel transforming cultures... In this sense, Christians are obsessed with the bad in others, and overlook the good in others, thus, forms the psychological barriers."[30] Ya-Tang Chuang has aptly remarks that Song's story theology aims at avoiding the dichotomy between gospel and cultures and overcoming the psychological barrier which is within us, Christians.[31] This is clearly understood in the light of what we understand by cultures and gospel mean for Song, both are inextricably related.

3.3.1.6. Story theology as People's Hermeneutics

The story theology Song practices is a form of people's hermeneutics. It is called people hermeneutics because it deals with people as the *locus* to interpret the meaning of the Bible, an understanding about the personhood of Jesus, and the significance of Jesus' message of the reign of God. It is considered as the most appropriate for Christian theology, the fact that Jesus himself practiced it. For Song, people are the locus in Jesus' experience of what God is like and what God is doing in the world—not people as an idea, a genus, a statistic, but as women, men and children disinherited, exploited, and marginalized.

---

[28] C.S. Song, "Story is the Matrix...," 38.

[29] Ya-Tang Chuang, "Practicing Contextual ...," 147.

[30] Ya-Tang Chuang, "Practicing Contextual ...," 147.

[31] Ya-Tang Chuang, "Practicing Contextual...," 148.

It is a living hermeneutics—hermeneutics not developed as a theory, but hermeneutics that grows out of the experiences of those people living in fear, deprivation and uncertainty. It is also a hermeneutic that inspires people to hope, strengthens them in faith, and empowers them to love.[32]

People's hermeneutics has its theological roots. It is possible only in its overcoming of the two dichotomies of gospel and cultures. Therefore, for Song, gospel is nothing but the story of Jesus, and the story of Jesus is none other than the story of how Jesus lives with-for-and-in the people. For Song, cultures packed with stories of people imply or contain the revelation of God and elements of salvation. Song is of the view that since culture is never empty, there is gospel implied in it and waiting for theologians to speak it out. Thus, in the light of this overcoming the two dichotomy business, Song does not intend any theologian to use gospel to destroy his/her own culture, nor does he want anyone to use gospel to transform it. But what is intended in Song's story theology is, "to penetrate with a keen heart and humble spirit, into the stories, (especially folk stories which is familiar to most people) in order to meet the Spirit of God that moves in his/her own culture."[33] Thus, the idea of transforming the society or culture does not come in here but to penetrate with keen heart. People hermeneutics does away abstract theological principles or set of doctrines, not even from the Bible itself. Rather, it begins with the real problems of the people and then allows these contexts to interact with the biblical texts. It begins with the stories of the people, and then re-tells the biblical stories in relation to these stories on the other hand, re-tells these stories in relation to the biblical stories. In practicing people hermeneutic, the authority of the Bible containing readymade answers to the puzzling questions of life does not arise. However, it has the authority to challenge us to open ourselves to God in order to open ourselves to the people.[34]

---

[32] Ya-Tang Chuang, "Practicing Contextual…," 149.

[33] Ya-Tang Chuang, "Practicing Contextual… " 149.

[34] Ya-Tang Chuang, "Practicing Contextual…," 151.

3.4. Asian Stories and Biblical Stories in Reciprocation

Song is crucial about Asian context that consists of an abundance of myths and stories of creation, often supreme in their poetic forms, profound in religious insights, and resplendent in their power of imagination. Like the creation story in the first two chapters of the Bible, which went through the influence of Babylonian creation epic of *Enuma Elish*, in the same vein, Song also comes up with the creation story of the Maoris of New Zealand in that *Io* causes light to shine in the darkness of the universe that runs parallel with the biblical creation accounts.

> *Io* dwelt within breathing-space of immensity.
> The universe was in darkness, with water everywhere.
> There was no glimmer of dawn, no clearness, no light.
> And he began by saying these words,
> That he might cease remaining inactive,
> "Darkness, become a light-possessing darkness."
> And at once light appeared.
> He then repeated those self-same words in this manner,
> That he might cease remaining inactive,
> "Light become a darkness-possessing darkness..."
> And again intense darkness supervened.
> Then a third time he spake, saying,
> "Let there be a darkness above,
> Let there be a darkness below...
> Let there be one light above,
> Let there be one light below...
> A dominion of light, A bright light."
> And now a great light prevailed.
> *Io* then looked to the waters which compassed him
> About and spake a fourth time, saying,
> "Ye waters of Tai-kama, be ye separate.
> Heavens be formed."
> Then the sky became suspended.

> "Bring forth thou Tu-pu-koro-nuka."
> And at once the moving earth lay stretch abroad.[35]

The Faithful Lady Meng is another folktale from which Song relates with the political ethic of the cross of Jesus.

> This happened in the reign of the wicked, unjust Emperor Ch'in Shih Huang-ti. He was afraid at this time that the Huns would break into the country from the north and not leave him any peace.
>
> Then a wise (!) man said to him: "A wall like this, which is over ten thousand miles long, can be built only if you immure a human being in every mile of the wall. Each mile will then have its guardian." It was easy for the Emperor to follow this advice, for he regarded his subjects as so much grass and weeds, and the whole land began to tremble under this threat.
>
> In order to keep them in check, he decided to build a wall along the whole northern frontier of China. But no sooner was one piece built than another fell down, and the wall made no progress.
>
> Plans were then made for human sacrifice in great numbers. At the last minute "an ingenious scholar" suggested to the Emperor that it would be sufficient to sacrifice a man called Wan "since Wan means ten thousand." Soldiers were dispatched at once to seize Wan who was sitting with his bride at the weeding feast. He was carried off by the heartless soldiers, leaving Lady Meng, his bride, in tears.
>
> Eventually, heedless of the fatigues of the journey, she travelled over mountains and through rivers to find the bones of her husband. When she saw the stupendous wall she did not know how to find the bones. There was nothing to be done, and she sat down and wept. Her

---

[35] Choan-Seng Song, *Theology from the Womb of Asia* (London: SCM Press Ltd., 1988), 9-10.

> weeping so affected the wall that it collapsed and laid bare her husband's bones.
>
> When the emperor heard of Meng Chiang and how she was seeking her husband, he wanted to see her himself. When she was brought before him, her unearthly beauty so struck him that he decided to make her Empress. She knew she could not avoid her fate, and therefore she agreed on three conditions. First, a festival lasting forty-nine days should be held in honour of her husband; second, the Emperor, with all his officials, should be present at the burial; and third, he should build a terrace forty-nine feet high on the bank of the river, where she wanted to make a sacrifice to her husband…Ch'in Shih Huang-ti granted all her request at once.
>
> When everything was ready she climbed on to the terrace and began to curse the Emperor in a loud voice for all his cruelty and wickedness. Although, this made the Emperor very angry, he held his peace. But when she jumped from the terrace into the river, he flew into a rage and ordered his soldiers to cut up her body into little pieces and grind her body to powder. When they did this, the little pieces changed into little silver fish, in which the soul of faithful Lady Meng Chiang lives for ever.[36]

Through this folktale Song affirms that folktales contain theological and political insights. He stresses that the kind of political theology found in the folktales can be more genuine, more powerful, more heartening than many Christian political theologies. Folktale political theology, says Song, is conceived in the womb of people's experience. "In the darkness of that womb a new life is hatched in people's tears and laughter; it struggles to grow in people's hope and despair,"[37] states Song. He says further "The source of our political theology in Asia is the people—the people humiliated, oppressed

[36] C.S. Song, *Tears of Lady Meng: A Parable of People's Political Theology* (Geneva: The Risk Book Series, 1981), 25-27.

[37] C.S. Song, *Tears of Lady Meng*, 29.

and impoverished. And the power of our political ethic comes from people's tears—tears of people shed because of their misery and the misery of others. People capable of crying, people capable of being moved to weep—this is the source and power of our political theology."[38] Through the story of Tears of Lady Meng, Song reads and re-tells the theology of Lady Meng as the theology of people. Song tells the story of Lady Meng as the story of Jesus because Song sees Jesus in suffering people, furthermore, Jesus as the "crucified people."[39] Song sees God is moved to tears, Jesus is moved to tears, the Buddha is moved to tears and people are moved to tears. Thus, a vital aspect of political theology is grasped here.[40] The tears of Lady Meng, Jesus and Buddha are deemed to represent the tears of the people or mass in Asia. Hence, Asian stories provide the most relevant point of entry for dialogue with Asian Christian theology.

Another story "Tell Us Our Names," extracted from the book, *Tell Us Our Names: Story Theology from an Asian Perspective* Song exemplifies the importance of naming the names, or the ability to pronounce the names of kith and kin correctly.[41] It took several days for a woman to pronounce her brothers-in-laws' names correctly.

---

[38] C.S. Song, *Tears of Lady Meng,* 43.

[39] Kyounghee Shin (Union-PSCE), "Theological Truth of Folk-Tales and Christian Education through an analysis of C. S. Song's Story Theology" old. religious education. net/proceedings/Shin_Theological, 13-12-2011.

[40] C.S. Song, *Tears of Lady Meng,* 43.

[41] Tell us our Names! A young man had four brothers. He met a girl and married her. The bride slept the four days of brideship. Then she went out of the house and set a pot of gruel on the fire. She cooked the gruel until it was done. She took out a plateful for her husband, and four platefuls for her brothers-in-law. She went to bring the food to them.

Her brothers-in-law said to her, "If we eat this gruel, tell us our names."

She said, "I do not know your names."

They said, "If you do not know our names, take away the gruel."

She took it up and went with it to her house. The husband and wife ate the gruel.

The same thing happened the next day. The woman was thinking to herself, "My brothers-in-law refuse to eat my gruel. But I do not know their names."

(Several days after, she was able to pronounce their names through the singing of the bird).

Her brothers-in-laws did not eat her gruel until she was able to pronounce their names correctly. This is to signify the importance of name-giving power. Song asserts that giving names to others—"to other human beings, animals, insects, birds, flowers, trees and a host of other things—is a prerogative of human beings. The ability to name is a sign of human nature. We Christians consider it a God-given ability. We have a proof of it in our Bible."[42] Adam was the first man whom God entrusted to name the created beings on earth and heavens (Genesis 2:19-20). The place of human beings in the world as name–givers is divinely ordained. No other creature can challenge it or take it away from them.[43] Thus, Song, in the light of this biblical evidence, denounces those Christian missions or missionaries and evangelists who christened persons or people whom they had won and territories they had conquered. One such example is reflected in the life of African man called Mangombe, meaning 'one who owns a large herd of cattle.' But after becoming Christian he was a baptized Charles, and his wife, Pfumai, meaning "may thou be wealthy," was given a Christian name so called Helen. Song ironically retaliates that Charles has nothing to do with Mangombe while the former is a perfectly good name that describes interdependent relationships that hold human being and animals together in a community. Song states, "It also serves as a link between past generations and future generations. It is not just the name of an individual. It is the name of the family, of tribe, of a people. In that name lives a history and in that name past, present and future converge."[44] Thus, names consist of a particular meaning and play a vital role in Asia and Africa respectively. In this case, Mangombe as Charles ceased to be a link in the family pedigree. He was cut off from his tribe, his people and his history.[45] Song while citing from a biblical text points

---

The woman said, "This one is Tumba Sikundu; this one, Tumba Sikundu Muna; this one, Tumba Kaulu; this one, Tumba Kaula Muna." Her brothers-in-law laughed. They accepted the gruel and ate it. C.S. Song, *Tell Us Our Names,* 89-90.

[42] C.S. Song, *Tell Us Our Names,* 90.

[43] C.S. Song, *Tell Us Our Names,* 90.

[44] C.S. Song, *Tell Us Our Names,* 92.

[45] C.S. Song, *Tell Us Our Names,* 93.

out, unlike Christian mission dispensing Christian names that turn into a nobody, Jesus was preoccupied with turning nobodies into somebody which is seen in his association with the undesirables (Matt.15:21-31). Song says, "What Christian mission should have is not the name-giving power but the name-knowing power—the power to identify names, the power to pronounce them correctly, and the power to understand and experience their deep meanings."[46] Song, through this folktale, "Tell Us Our Names" brings us to our cognizance that our response determines our place in the community whether we are insider or outsider, a visitor or a family member, alien or a citizen in our attitude towards society. Thus, pronouncing and understanding names correctly, and not name-giving authority, is an integral part of Asian community life. So, if taken Song's perspective, those were the missionaries who were not endowed with name-giving power, rather they were the people who should be able to identify each and every particular unique culture of others and call them accordingly as given. To be critical about it, God did not send them to establish Welsh Mission, Baptist Mission, Presbyterian Mission or Catholic Mission alike except that they go and let the gospel incarnate in people's culture.

3.5. Evaluation of Song's Story Theology

The propagation of using sources outside Christianity such as cultures and stories for Christian theology is intrinsically associated with Song's understanding of the relationship between archetype and types. He understands each type of stories is *sui-generis,* an original type, an archetype. It means no type of story is sub-type of another type or an archetype. There is no need to regard a particular type as archetype over other types as normative.[47] Although, Song never means biblical stories as unimportant yet he considers the Bible as a type in itself and not as archetype for other cultures and religions. He advocates "interaction" of gospel and cultures. In order to do that he advocates the idea of relational that human being is relational

[46] C.S. Song, *Tell Us Our Names,* 93.

[47] C. S. Song, "Doing Theologies with Stories Theological Education, Where Do We Go," 16.

being as God in creation has all things, animate and inanimate, inseparably interrelated. Likewise, in its natural sense, Christians are to interrelate to other cultures, others, nature, religions, dialogue of any kind.[48] It is through the perspective of "relational" that Song advocates an interaction between the biblical and Asian stories, this truth has been revealed to us in the studies of ecosystems, i.e. everything is interdependent.

Song sees story theology as a theological movement originated in Jesus and carried out by him against the prevailing tradition of his contemporary teachers and believers. According to him, stories precede and correct doctrines, doctrines rewrite and distort stories. He sees "story theology" as a credible biblical and theological method. Jesus' method is method of confessing faith and doing theology with stories and not with doctrines.[49] Stories are energized by life force to be born, to live, and to make impacts on the life and minds of readers, while doctrines are developed by the power that dominates and intimidates people.[50] Whether edifying or destructive, good or evil stories, they engage us in faith and theology. Stories are media through which edifying and destructive stories, good and evil are told from one generation to another. Those were the stories of Jesus that motivated many people and inspired them to challenge evil powers and changed the course of history. Thus, story theology is transformative, liberative to people from status quo, be it religious, cultural, social or political whereas doctrines are conformative, and they force them to conform to it. Story theology liberates and transforms people's lives that are kept captive by traditions and doctrines of the church.[51] Story theology breaks through fundamentalism and traditionalism of faith and theology.[52] Such being the case, what Asian Christian theology needs to do is, breakthrough the garb of traditionalism, status quo and fanaticism

[48] C. S. Song, "Doing Theologies...," 17.

[49] C. S. Song, "Doing Theologies...," 10.

[50] C. S. Song, "Doing Theologies...," 11.

[51] C. S. Song, "Doing Theologies...," 15.

[52] C. S. Song, "Doing Theologies...," 9.

found in the church practices but learn how to be relational and transformative with every people's cultures and worldviews.

He is of the view that the church does not have any mission of its own except God's only mission of redeeming and liberating both the oppressed and the oppressors. Therefore, if God's mission is the mission of suffering, then, the church has no other mission except God's mission. The Christian mission is designated for Christians to suffer with the oppressed in struggling for justice and freedom. This vision of the mission grows out of the reality of the Asian people. Song finds the Christian church in the season of distress and adjustment: distress because the ambition of "Christianizing" the world is not fulfilled, and adjustment because its centuries-old life-view and world-view have become obsolete and new ones have to be constructed. Song is of the view that the future of Christianity cannot be separated from the future of other religions, that the well-being of the Christian church is closely bound with the well-being of the larger community around it, and that Christians and their neighbours are fellow pilgrims on earth in search of the meaning of life and the fulfilment of it.[53] Such being the case, the issue of evangelization or conversion, baptism, establishing of the churches does not arise here. Rather it drives us on to be "salt and light" of the world.

3.6. Conclusion

Kyounghee Shin extracting from Song's book, *Jesus, the Crucified People*, states, "If you want to know God, we must turn to humanity that is, to our neighbour, for God loves and is close to our neighbour. *Theo*-logical questions are in reality *anthropo*-logical questions."[54] The subject matter of theology is not something an abstract thing alone but basically it has to do with socio-politico-cultural and ecological aspects of human beings the fact that it is not possible to get a glimpse of divine reality without going through these human

[53] C. S. Song, "Christian Theology: Towards an Asian Reconstruction" in http://www.religion-online.org/showarticle.asp?title=128 (09.12.2011).

[54] Kyounghee Shin (Union-PSCE), "Theological Truth of Folk-Tales and Christian Education through an analysis of C. S. Song's Story Theology" old. religious education. net/proceedings/Shin_Theological, 13-12-2011.

realities. Song, in all his theological dealings with Asian resources such as folk literature, history, religion and story theology, has touched the nucleus of human realities in Asia. He has not disregarded any of cultures, religions or worldview. The folktales which Song brings out from different religious and cultural contexts have expressed similar views with the stories found in the Bible. Likewise, the Kuki in particular has a lot more to do with folktales, legends myth etc. in the light of Song's theology of cultures, especially Song's story theology has much to share with the Kuki culture of myths, legends, folktales and the social ethical system. In this regard, Song has rightly pointed out that there is no race, community or tribe that has no folktales, myth, legends etc. thus, the Kuki cultural context will be discussed relationally with Song's theology of cultures or story theology successively.

Chapter 4

The Kuki Socio-Religious-Cultural Context: An Overview

4.1. Introduction

Having explored Song's theology of cultures in the three preceding chapters, now we will move on to the Kuki cultural context and some tribals of Northeast India in general. Culture and tradition are elements that preserve people's identity which distinguish people from one another. As has already been remarked that for Song, culture is human beings as individuals, as member of a family and a society, as men and women, and children related to one in a human community.[1] Correspondingly, the Kuki culture, in a complex matter of socio-political, religious and cultural aspects, is a binding force where every individual of the community is inevitably related to one another. Failing to relate to the whole complex of culture may result to chaos. Therefore, in this chapter, the focus is on the Kuki tribal cultures of communitarian value system, social ethics, land and the Supreme Being and its theological validation.

[1] Ya-Tang Chuang, "Gospel and Cultures...," 6.

4.2. A Brief History of the Kukis, its Origin, Migration and Settlement

4.2.1. Origin and Migration

The Thadou-Kuki traces back their progenitor to Chongthu/ Chawngthu who was believed to have born during B.C. 250 and said to have come out of the bowels of the earth called *Khul* (cave)[2] which is analogous to Sinlung and Chinlung versions, the location is believed by some to be somewhere in China, but others claim it to be in Tibet.[3] `According to M. Mucculoh, as quoted by M. Thongkhosei Haokip, a king's brother, while hunting hedge-hodge with his dog entered a cavern and when his dog did not return, he went inside and found himself on the surface of the earth. According to William Shaw, upon the discovery of the surface of the earth, Chongthu (a relative of *Noimangpa*-Lord of subterranean) conjured up his ideas of forming a village of his own on the surface of that earth. So, during a feast performed by Noimangpa, Chongthu intentionally waved his sharp sword so vigorously in his dancing that he injured some of the folk present that angered them and the king. Consequently, he was ordered to be killed and he and his followers started to prepare to their escape.[4] Despite the different accounts with respect to location, however it is generally accepted that the Kukis came out of *khul* (cave). Although, the exact location is not known but some suggested *khul* to be in Sechwan province of China and Sinlung or Chhinlung as their original home that is strongly supported by songs and legends that have been handed down from generation to generation. This has been testified by ancient folk song that is still sung:

> My chin land of old
> My grandfather's land Himalei (Himalayas)

---

[2] T. S. Gangte, *Structure of Thadou Society* (Thadou te Hungkonna Thusim le Aphunggui ju Thusim), translated and introduced by Dr. D. Singson (Imphal: Dr. D. Singson, 2003), 2.

[3] T. S. Gangte, *The Kukis of Manipur: A Historical Analysis* (New Delhi: Gyan Publishing House, 1993), 14 – 16.

[4] M. Haokhothong Haokip, *Ecumenism*, 41.

My grandfather's way excels
Chhinlung's (Chin rock) way excels.[5]

It was also generally believed that the Kukis migrated from China during the reign of Chinese Emperor Chinglung or Chie'nlung, around 200 B.C. Another Mizo historian Zawla claimed that the Kukis came out of Great Wall of China in about 225 B.C. during the reign of Shih Hungti who was at time so cruel. The two accounts are but without any written evidence to support them.[6] However, another historian Enriquez claimed to have an ample scientific data to prove that the Tibeto-Burman group comprising Pyu-Burmese-Kachin, Kuki-Chin and Lolo initially moved towards the West and thereafter subdivided themselves into several groups. They followed different routes, one group reaching Tibet on the North where some of them stayed behind, while others moved on Northwards until they reached Burma in three waves. These people were the Kuki-Chin and the Pyu-Burmese-Kachin. The Kuki-Chin group moved further towards South-West following the Irrawady and Chindwin rivers and continued to move until they reached the shores of the Bay of Bengal.[7]

4.2.2. Settlement

Presently the Kukis are settled in Nagaland, the Province of Myanmar in the east, Mizoram in the south and the District of Cachar in the West. Mainly, it may be said, they occupy the hills of the state of Manipur on all sides of the Imphal valley[8] and the Bawm people also in the Chittagong Hill Tracts in Bangladesh represent Kuki.[9] The denomination 'Kuki-Chin' is a purely conventional one and the

---

[5] M. Haokhothong Haokip, *Ecumenism*, 41.

[6] T. S. Gangte, *The Kukis of Manipur*, 17.

[7] T. S. Gangte, *The Kukis of Manipur*, 18.

[8] William Shaw, *Notes on the Thadou Kukis* edited with Introduction, Notes, Appendices, Illustrations and Index by J. H. Hutton (Delhi: Spectrum Publication, 1997), 11.

[9] The Kuki group in Chittagong Hill Tracts are Tlangmi or hill people (they are Bawm, Pangkhua, Lushai, Khumi, Mro, Khyang). Seikholen Haokip, *Rhetorics of the Kuki Nationalism: A Treatise* (New Delhi: Lustra Print, 2010), 18.

words Kuki and Chin are synonymous and are both used for many of the hill tribes.[10]

M. Thongkhosei Haokip in his analysis of the history of the Kukis, he has neatly classified into three phases: Pre-British, the British Period and After India's Independence. Under the Pre-British Period, by the name 'Kuki' before 19th century was never heard of. The word 'Kuki' first appeared in the pages of history in AD 1830 with the writing of Sir James Johnstone. However, this does not mean that there were no Kukis in the land. Rather it does mean that the Kukis then were known after the names of their villages, or chiefs, clan names or even by peculiar references used by others. Thus, prior to Pakhangba (the king of Moirang from 90 BC-AD 30), the Kukis appeared to have been known as Chingburoi, owner or master of the Hills. "The stories of different Kuki tribes like Milhiem, Chothe, etc., prove that the Kukis are the true aborigines of Manipur."[11] They were also known as Haos.[12] Later the term Khogsai appears to have found in its usage.

> Between AD 264 and 364, the king of Mulpi (Joupi) Kaikholun's son adopted by King Khoi called Taothingmang reigned as king of Manipur for a period of 100 years. It is said that the Meitiei-sub nation came into being out of the Kuki race since the reign of Meidingu Naothingkho Meitrabak from 670 AD. Naothingkho wanted to unite the nine petty kings and their clans, and

---

[10] G. A. Grierson, *Linguistic Survey of India*, vol. III, Tibeto-Burman Family part III, Kuki-Chin and Burma Groups (Delhi: Low Price Publication,1990), 1.

[11] M. Thongkhosei Haokip, *Ecumenism*, 43.

[12] In the Moirang pre-history, Chothe Thangvai Pakhangba, known as Ivang Purik Lai Thingri Nachousa, ruled for 120 years (BC 90-30AD). About 33 AD, during the reign of King Nongda Laren Pakhangba, a man named Poireton came to Manipur with ambitions of becoming a king. He mustered the support of many chieftains from the hills (who were apparently the Kukis) and declared war on Pakhangba. He was unable to win the war, but managed to extract an honourable treaty by which the king of Manipur married the younger sister of Poireton, and Poireton and his followers were assimilated into the kingdom with Poireton himself becoming the Prime Minister. After his arrival, the Kukis came to be known as Haos. M. Thongkhosei Haokip, *Ecumeinism*, 42-43.

> in pursuit to this end, married the daughters of four kings of the hill tribes of Siloi Langmai, Khumen, Moirang and Mangang. These matrimonial and the resultant process of assimilation contributed a great deal in restoration of peace and establishment of a Meitei nation in the valley. From AD 984 to 1079 King Irengba integrated those Kukis wishing to become Meiteis under the banner of "Poirei Meitei" which is said to have composed of two-thirds of the present Meiteis which is well illustrated in the Meitei ritual of *Sagei Khunthok lon.*[13]

Further it is observed by P. S. Haokip, that Meitei dialect belongs to the Kuki language family. He quoted that the linguistic survey of India Vol. III Pt. II also classifies Meitei as a Kuki dialect. So, it is to the fact that of all the Bengali and Hindi words removed from Meitei *lon*, all that remain are the Kuki language.[14]

4.2.3. Theological Significance of the Kuki History

As per tradition and historical evidences are concerned, we are informed that they were enslaved and treated cruelly by the king of China imposing stiff work upon the Kuki ancestors for the accomplishment of his selfish desire and vested interest in constructing 'the Great wall of China.' Their exodus was not without reasons; they had genuine stories to tell us of their pains, hardships, which were intolerable, indeed beyond human tolerance. The history and tradition evidenced that there was divine intervention to their escape. Yahweh of Israel was not only for the people of Israel but He was also the God of the Kuki ancestors. God could not tolerate the pains and sufferings of the ancient Kuki community when they were subjected to hard work and cruel treatment by the task master in the land where they had their settlement. It was the same God of Israel who brought them out of their oppressed situation. The compassionate God, who moves on the surface of the earth, also moves alongside the sufferings of the ancient Kuki community, not only to Israel because God is a God of every

[13] M. Thongkhosei Haokip, *Ecumenism*, 44.

[14] M. Thongkhosei Haokip, *Ecumenism*, 44.

creation and of the world. Absolutizing God's movement within some particular location is theological fallacy. The God who suffered alongside the enslaved Israelites, too, suffered with the ancient Kuki community. God in His due time intervened through the person of their progenitor Chongthu to a far-enriching place, a promised land where they would live in a land of freedom.

When Chongthu/Chawngthu and his party came out of the bowels of the earth called *Khul* (cave), their journey was not without hindrances. Tradition says,

> As they marched towards *Khulkot* (entrance of the cave), they saw a *giant* python, GULLHEOPI blocking their path. It had beaten some to death with its long tail. Pu Chongthu wrapped his head with *phoipi* (a thick blanket-like cloth) and risked life for his people. With *joudichem* (sword) confronted the giant snake and sliced it to seven pieces. They safely passed through and continued their journey towards *Khulkot.*[15]

As they made their move further, they encountered a big and ferocious lion that stood on their path again. Since Pu Chongthu was a man of wits and knowledge, he politely spoke to the lion, "Hasn't God made you ruler of over all animals? If it is so, God has made me ruler over all humankind. Let us not make a row, but make an alliance and be friends…hearing this, the lion did not harm to him, but silently walked away."[16] The story goes on stating that the journey all through they made had been life-threatening events. Further the tradition says,

> On reaching Khulkot, they found it was closed with a huge boulder. Vangal came to their aid. It heaved and lifted the boulder and let the whole team pass through it. Pu Chongthu's elder brother, Pu Chongja and some others were far behind. It was because Pi Nemneh, the wife of Pu Chongja returned to get her *nih* (petty-coat) but some

---

[15] Hatjaphal (Phalsi), *History Behind Kuki Folk Dances and Lores*, (Dimapur: Gospel Printing Press, 2018), 10.

[16] Hatjaphal (Phalsi), *History Behind*, 10.

> said, *dumdip* (small bag for holding tobacco). When they reached Khul-kot, it was already closed by Vangal. They could not open it. So Pi Nemneh flew into fiery anger and cursed Pu Chongthu and his party.[17]

Pi Nemneh's curse runs thus alongside free translation:

> Thi leh manin juijun; nat le satnin juijun
> (Death and loss be after you; sorrows and diseases be with you)[18]

Following their migration from the bondage of *Khul*, Pu Chongthu celebrated their historic escape from *Khul* through folklore called *Khulla* that authenticates the real historical events. The lore runs alongside free translation:

> Thampi Khulla ka penni hinno (When I was born in Khul)
> Tengpi sonlha ka kitoi; (I walked with my spear and sword)
> Khul kot dongpi ka hongnge (opened the entrance of khul)
> ka nung teng mitin twi banga alonge (behind all flowed like a river)[19]

Theologically what is crucial to us in the light of Song theology of cultures is that every history, culture and religion is equally important as the history, religion and culture of Israel. Every people's experience is unique and valid in its own way. Hence no people's experience, be it history, culture or religion, should be subjected to the history, culture and religion of Israel as point of reference for normative judgment. Song has rightly observed that each type of stories is *sui-generis,* an original type, an archetype. It means no type of story is sub-type of another type or an archetype.[20] There is no need to regard a particular type as archetype over other types as normative. So, the exodus movement of the Kuki ancestors cannot be deemed as second hand experience compared to the Exodus movement of Israel in any degree.

---

[17] Hatjaphal (Phalsi), *History Behind,* 10-11.

[18] Hatjaphal (Phalsi), *History Behind,* 11.

[19] Hatjaphal (Phalsi), *History Behind,* 11.

[20] C. S. Song, "Doing Theologies...,"11.

The Kuki ancestors went through piles of obstacles in the same way as the people of Israel did on their way to Promised Land. The same God of Israel was with them in all their struggles and toils. When people suffer, God, too, suffers. For Song, God in Jesus is a God who suffers with people in suffering. Jesus, in short, is the suffering and crucified people. However, this God is not only a God of suffering but also a God of hope. The powerlessness of Jesus has been transformed into the powerfulness of the Christ. Such a powerful God is able to liberate the people who suffer from the power of death[21] and give new life. So, the God who was with the Kuki ancestors is and will continue to be the God of their descendants amidst the pains and struggles in their present settlement.

4.3. Impact of Western Christianity on Kuki Tribal Religious and Cultural Traditions

In spite of the fact that Christianity has its positive impacts upon the Kuki people and tribals as a whole such as `liberation work carried out in the form of education, printing press, hospitals, translations of scripture and many more,[22] yet the Christians at present age cannot be uncritical of its impact in the long run. Christianity of westernized form has caused tremendous problem in the Kuki community. Loss of culture has caused tremendous problems to self-identification among the Kuki community. The unification of a nation largely depends indispensably on their common cultural heritage. To this fact of social philosophy, the Kukis have abandoned their religious tradition, custom and culture which serve as a binding cord. As far as the unification of the people is concerned, the present Christianity is unable to meet the need of the people.[23] Loss of tribal spirituality; this spirituality cannot be conceived without being related to space

---

[21] http://people.bu.edu/wwildman/bce/song.htm, (09/04/2019).

[22] Wait Longchar, "The continuity of Indigenous people in Today's World," in *Theologizing Tribal Heritage: A Critical Re-Look*, edited by Hrangthan Chhungi (Delhi: CWM/ISET-ECC/PCI/ISPCK, 2008), 65.

[23] Dongkhothang Singson "A Critical Appraisal of the Coming of Christianity Among the Kuki of Manipur," in *An Emerging Tribal Theology from Kuki Perspective*, edited by L. Seikholen (Imphal: Trulock Theological Seminary, 2011), 18.

or land[24] because the land or earth is the basis of all realities—human selfhood, no clear cut between sacred and secular, all religious activities are earth-centered, Sacred Power comes from the soil, so on and so forth[25] because anything that does not conform to the western worldview were considered devilish, irrational inhuman, backward, primitive and so forth. As such tribal religion is considered without any system of thought, devoid of morality and spirituality by the missionaries, colonizers, students of anthropology so on and so forth.[26] There is confusion due to compartmentalization of every walk of people's life such as socio-cultural, political and religious aspects that are typical in the western value system, and are quite alien to the tribals who are homogeneous in every aspect of life.[27] Due to this uprootedness from the primal religious traditions and cultural practices, social injustice, corruptions, political instability, economic deterioration and dependency, religion and moral laxity, interdenominational divisions, ethnic conflicts, rise of terrorism or insurgency movements are rampant.[28]

4.4. Prevailing Social and Cultural Ethics

Like rest of many other communities, there are certain social ethics in the Kuki tribal culture without which such communitarian way of life cannot be practiced. This principle of philosophy is called *tomngaina* in Kuki, *tlawmngaihna* by the Mizos and *sobaliba* by the Ao Nagas. However, with the coming of Christianity alongside with its modernization and globalization, a long cherished value such as *tomngaina*, which is one of the constituents of cultures, is largely eroded. Prof. Lal Dena has rightly observed this:

---

[24] A. Wati Longcahr, *An Emerging Asian Theology: Tribal Theology: Issue, Method and Perspective* (Jorhat: Tribal Study Centre Eastern Theological College, 2000), 65.

[25] Wait Longchar, "The Continuity of Indigenous…," 65.

[26] A. Wati Longchar, *The Tribal Religious Traditions in North East India: An Introduction* (Jorhat: Eastern Theological College, 2000), 6.

[27] Letkhothang Haokip, "The Interaction Between the Kuki Religion and Christian in North East India," in *An Emerging Tribal Theology from Kuki Perspective*, 7.

[28] Letkhothang Haokip, "The Interaction…," 7-8.

> Modernization and globalization has greatly affected the indigenous peoples worldwide. Throughout North-east India, we are witnessing the widespread removal of traditional activities and the family-community setting; the altered family-structure in the face of the changing labour market; the increased drifting apart of children from family and home on the pretext of higher education; the decline of parental authority since schools have replaced the family as the primary educational unit; moral degeneration; diminishing reverence for elders because they are no longer the repositories of knowledge with the intrusion of the print media replacing oral tradition and exploitation of the natural environment.[29]

Closely related to *tomngaina* is *khankho*, way of life wherein attempt is made to understand these ethical principles relatively and not as a totally separate entity from other aspects. *Tlawmngaihna*[30] is also the social principle as well as the norm for good conduct of the people in the community. The tribal moral ethos is based on good deeds for the welfare of the community by putting first the interest of the community over against individual interest.[31] *Tlawmngaihna* embraces various types of human qualities and activities, and manifests itself in various forms and aspects of community life, which is best summed up as "community over self." The Mizo code of ethics revolves around *tlawmngaihna*.[32] Thanzauva feels quite similar the Ao Nagas' concept of *sobaliba* with that of the Mizo's *tlawmngahna.*

---

[29] http://proflaldena.blogspot.com/2014/10/selected-mizo-folk-tales-reading-in.html (26/03/19).

[30] *Tomngaina/Tlawmngaihna* is a life philosophy, carnal virtue and practice of the (Kuki) Mizo people. It has no equivalent word in English for translation; it basically means 'self-less service rendered to the needy people without any hope of reward." It is the life principle that binds the village community together and turns the stiff hills terrains into paradise for the dwellers. Rev. Khuanga, "The Role of Christianity in the Socio-Economic Praxis of Mizoram," in *Towards a Tribal Theology: The Mizo Perspective* (Jorhat: The Mizo Theological Conference, 1989), 97.

[31] K. Thanzauva, *Theology of Community: Tribal Theology in the Making* (Aizawl: Mizo Theological Conference, 1997), 122.

[32] K. Thanzauva, *Theology of Community,* 123.

According to A. Wati Longchar *Sobaliba*[33] in Ao Naga connotes the same meaning with the term *tomngaina/tlawmngaihna. Sobaliba* is a special ethical gift on human bestowed by the Supreme Creator. This special gift is bestowed on human beings so that respect, care and protection of fellow creatures from destruction may be executed out. Through the practice of this ethical principle, human beings enter into communion with God and with all the rest of living and non-living things.[34] Thanzauva summarizes *sobaliba* as total surrender of one's life to the cause of the whole society.[35] A comparison between *tlawmngaihna* and *niskama karma* is also brought out by Thanzauva where he finds *niskama karma* not so much different in its teaching but it remains religious ideal without having much impact on the society.[36] Relatively, H. Chongloi uses *khankho* as an alternative term for *tomngaina.* Thus, it unthinkable for the Kukis to be unrelated with their culture especially the unseen and unwritten binding force so called *khankho* which is shown in **Chart No. 1**

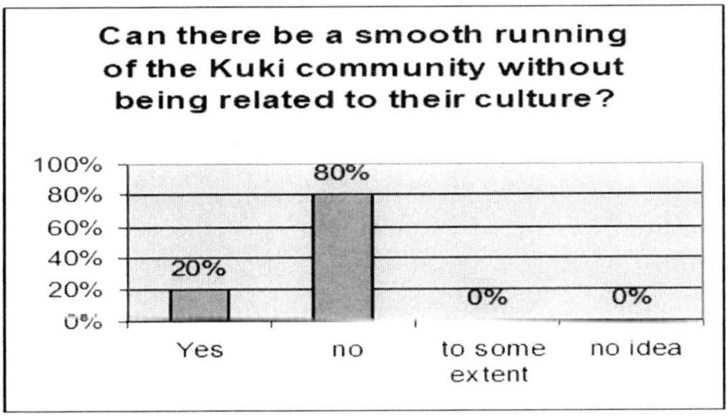

Chart No. 1[37]

[33] *Sobaliba* is an Ao Naga term of moral principle containing a wide range of implications for both individual and commuity life. It includes self-sacrifice, total self-denial, preservation, cooperation, honesty, truthfulness, industrious etc.

[34] A. Wati Longchar, *An Emerging Asian Theology,* 74.

[35] K. Thanzauva, *Theology of Community,* 125.

[36] K. Thanzauva, *Theology of Community,* 126.

[37] Empirical research was carried out both in the form of interview and questionnaire; the focused group was people between 30-72 ages, out of 220

What the Bible encourages us to be always industrious has a direct consonance with the social philosophy of the tribals. 2 Thessalonians 3:10 is one such instance "...Anyone unwilling to work should not eat." There are other several passages that disapprove being sluggish. Prof. Lal Dena has aptly delineates the term *tomngaina* as "A noble quality of keeping the others first and the 'self' second."[38] So within the concept of *tomngaina*, laziness is unheard of, there is dignity of labour and traditional people execute what is due to them at a given moment without hesitation, which means, priority is always given to others. This social philosophy would have closer consonance with the words of Jesus, "Just as the Son of Man came not be served but to serve, and to give his life a ransom for many," (Matt. 20:28). *Tomngaina*, when carried out appropriately in the social ambience of the tribal context, biblical mandate of the horizontal aspect is felt to have accomplished and naturally the social atmosphere is permeated with love, joy, peace, etc. which has sound consonance with the biblical teachings, "... the fruit of the Spirit is love, joy, peace, patience, patience, kindness, generosity, faithfulness, gentleness and self-control," (Gal. 5:22-23).

4.4.1. *Khankho*[39] (way of life)

In its appropriation of the term *Khankho* could mean 'the way a manner in which a person should grow up in the village or land,' or the manner in which a person should conduct himself or herself in life,' or 'the norms one adheres to while living in the village or land.'[40]

---

questionnaires distribution, 204 received. Interviews were done to 60 people. However only issues related to the thesis are employed. Among theological graduates, B.Th- D.Th = 20 people; Secular graduates, Bachelor Degree—Post Graduate= 70 people; Matriculation = 60 people; Under-matriculation=50 people. The same percentage applies in all charts hereafter.

[38] http://proflaldena.blogspot.com/2014/10/selected-mizo-folk-tales-reading-in.html (26/03/19).

[39] *Khankho* in its etymological breakup of the term may mean, khan=grow, deal, behave etc; and *kho*=village, land lifetime etc. When the two words are integrated into one word the resultant meaning undergoes a change, surpassing the meanings in their separate entities

[40] Hemchon Chongloi, "Khankhology...," 87.

It could also mean the principle on which the world is founded, which might be called the Sanskrit equivalent of Dharma.[41] The inclusiveness of the term and its wide ranging meaning of the concept could be grasped only in the context of the people's social, political, economic, cultural, religious and ethical life.[42] Hence, socio-political implication of *Khankho* administered by two sets of relationships that unite all members of the community, such as *Tucha-sunggao-becha-nulam* and *Upa-nao-pa* relationships can be explicated below.

4.4.1.1. *Tucha-Sunggao-Becha-Nulam* Reletionships

The institution of the *Becha*[43] and the *Tucha*[44] is a very important one in the Kuki family system. It is through the *Becha* and the *Tucha,* the family units maintain intimate and compact relationship between the families belonging to the different clans. A highly disciplined organizational setup for the observances of numerous social and religious functions is maintained through this institution of *Becha* and *Tucha*. The *Becha* and the *Tucha* may be considered as the friends, philosopher and guides of the Kuki families.[45] It is customarily mandatory that the younger married son has to establish his family consisting of *tucha* and *becha* through the initiative of the eldest brother (the father may be alive and be the initiator but the deed is credited to the eldest brother). Thus, the intricacies of the structure explicated by H. Chongloi through one reference point- Mr. X can be viewed.

> For him the *sunggao* relatives are already determined, they are the kinsmen of his mother. The mother's brother or son as *sunggao*

---

[41] Hemchon Chongloi, "Khankhology...," 87.

[42] Hemchon Chongloi, "Khankhology...," 87.

[43] The word *Becha* is a Kuki word. It denotes a person who is firmly attached to a family not his own. In short, the *Becha* performs the job of a general manager of the family shouldering the managerial responsibilities in all the social functions including the liaison work of the family. Without the *Becha* performances of any Kuki social function is unthinkable

[44] The institution of the *Tucha* is also very important and indispensable in the Kuki social system. In Kuki language nephews are called *Tu.*

[45] Tarun Goswami, *Kuki Life and Lore,* 19.

> is entitled to claim long-man (price of dead body) of X. *Sunggao* relatives are passive participants in their religious undertakings of X, contributing in kind whenever the stipulated, offering sound advice but they never involve directly in the family affairs of X. For X his eldest brother may appoint for him two or more *tuchas* one of which is the head *tucha*. They are taken from families who have procured brides from the family line of X. The head *tucha* is one closest in this bride giver-receiver reckoning. Two or more *bechas* for X are also appointed from families who are neither *tucha* nor *sunggao* relatives. The *bechas* are taken from any clan, but usually from X's clan members, for they are, especially the head *becha* becomes the spokesman for X in all his religio-social undertakings and decision-makings.[46]

Such relatives are framed on reciprocal basis. It is possible mainly because of the practice of marriage of mother's brother's daughter by way of preference, in such case, ego's children and the ego himself are *Tuchas* to his wife's parents, brother and brother's sons. If it is not mother's brother's daughter-marriage, an ego's children alone are *Tuchas* to his wife's parents, brother and brother's sons.[47] Although, the Kuki social structure represents patriarchy where the female folk seem to have no role in the kinship, yet certain social relationships are built on the female side which is called *Nulam. Nulam* is a term used for the relationship between households who have procured wives from the family. These households formed a close-knit unit in the social structure of the Kuki. Great importance is also given to the status of the women in the *sunggao* (mother's) relations as the recipient of *longman* (price of corpse) is reckoned on this relationship. The bond between the *tucha* and *sunggao* relationship is supposedly considered as the strongest in the Kuki kinship structure. For the Kuki to abide by, and function through this system is *khankho*.[48]

---

[46] Hemchon Chongloi, "Khankhology...," 87.

[47] T. S. Gangte, *The Kukis of Manipur*, 46.

[48] Hemkhochon Chongloi, *Indoi*, 131-132.

4.4.1.2. *Upa-Naopa* Relationships

The second set of relationship is hierarchical in the sense that it is reckoned from genealogical order. The relation is between *upa–naopa* (elder-younger per genealogical line). It has a range of levels of reckonings beginning at family level it progressively moves to levels of sub-clan, clan and eventually to the whole tribal confederation. Again the exposition of H. Chongloi is referred here from a reference point, Mr. X.

> He is the eldest of seven brothers, and therefore *upa* of six younger brothers. X's father is the younger of the two brothers. For X's the son of his father's elder brother becomes *upa*. But X's father and uncle are the sons of the person who has one elder brother and five younger brothers. Therefore the grandson of the above 'elder brother' becomes the *upa* of X as well as his immediate *upa*. This description involves three generations. The system however, may extend to the widest limit in which members of one whole clan members are *nao-pa* or *upa* in their reciprocal relationship with another clan members. Ultimately, there is one *upa* who is referred to as *Bulpi.*[49]

The whole populace is bound to the structure of *upa-naopa* relationship. This tribal confederation seems shaky outwardly but the thread that bound them to the structure is very strong. That thread is *khankho*, it stipulates what is expected of every individual to behave in relation to *upa* or *naopa*. This strong ethical bond enable them to withstand the onslaught of the mighty British aggression during the Anglo-Kuki war 1917-1919 into their loading muskets and indigenous snares at their disposal.[50] This patriarchal social

[49] *Bulpi*-by virtue of being the eldest in primordial time Doungel is *upa* of all sub-clans, therefore referred to as *bulpi* of these conglomerate clans. *Bulpi* and *u-pa* are synonymous in that they are chiefs of clans, but every upa cannot be *bulpi* whereas all *bulpi* are also *upa*. Hemchon Chongloi, "Khankhology A Study of the Socio-Political, Religio-Cultural Norms of the Kuki People," in *An Emerging Tribal Theology from Kuki Perspective,* 90.

[50] Hemchon Chongloi, "Khankhology...," 91.

system helps one to trace one's genealogical line accurately for many generations and maintains their *upa–naopa* hierarchical relationship. The present empirical data (**Chart No. 2**) shows decline of *khankho* due to the emergence of the new religion so called Christianity and modernization but it is not to be understood only in relation to *upa-naopa* relationship, here *khankho* as a whole may be thought of.

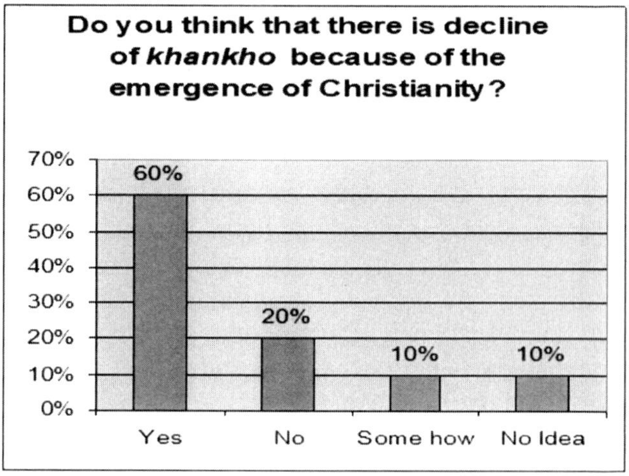

Chart No. 2

One cannot deny the fact of the Kuki cultural crisis began to ensue in the middle part of the 20th century that further resulted to mushrooming of Christian denominations among the people. Precisely, it failed to interpret the gospel into the cultural-social and philosophical thought forms of the people, the misconception that the new religion had nothing to do with their culture. K. S. Singson observes that it is due to the prior presentation of Christianity over Christ that cultural degradation was unavoidable.[51] Therefore, one could assume that the disintegration probably be due to religio-cultural clashes. The chart given below (**Chart No. 3**) would give us

[51] Personal interview with Rev. K. S. Singson, B. D., Kuki Christian Church, Nagaland Synod, on (12th of Dec. 2011), age 68, Ahthibung town, Peren Dist. Nagaland.

hints of how the cultural values are turned down with the emergence of Christianity. This is indicative of failure of the Christian missionaries to indigenously adopt the native culture and interpret the gospel in their cultural thought forms.

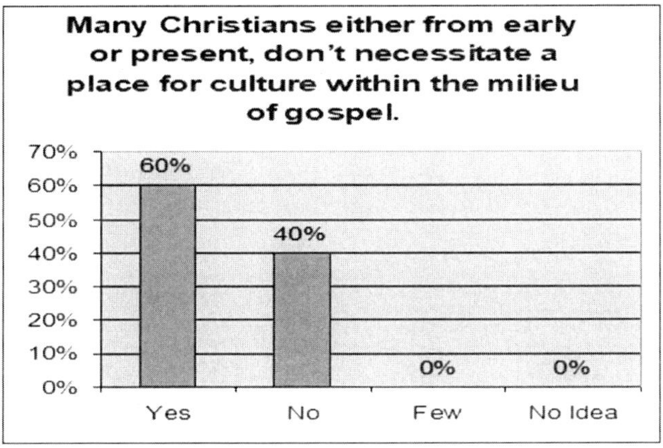

Chart No. 3

4.4.2. Theological Significance of *Khankho*

The whole ethical principles of the Kukis revolve around the system of *khankho* by which a Kuki is obliged to fulfil what is due to him/her at the religious, social and political levels.[52] The practice of *Khankho* as ethical principle of loving others as 'yourself' is the manifestation of the unseen Christ, and the presence of *Indoi* as a symbol of Loving God.[53] If fulfilling the two sets of right relationships; first is a vertical relationship between God and the human person and the second is horizontal relationship between human person and his/ her fellow human being and other creations.[54] Jesus' sum up of the Ten Commandments: "You shall love your neighbours as yourself"[55] can be seen as fulfilment of the aspired ethical vision of *khankho*

[52] Satkhokai Chongloi, "The Unseen Christ...," 142.

[53] Satkhokai Chongloi, "The Unseen Christ...," 140.

[54] Hemkhochon Chongloi, "Khankhology...,"95.

[55] Matthew 22:39; Mark 12:31: Luke 10:27.

which is condensed in the saying 'igol paipeh'a ihetle eima paipeh a akihenge' meaning, "If you first fill your friends' basket yours is also eventually filled."[56] Closely related to this is Jesus' command to make reconciliation among brothers before offering a gift at the altar.[57] Even the Psalmist longs for brothers and (sisters) to live in unity.[58] Yearning for reconciliation and unity among brothers and sisters is best explicated in *khankho*. This is to say *khankho* of social relationships are to be first set right. Another distinctive mark of God's kingdom on earth is the understanding of human beings as 'persons-in-community.' Relationship between individuals are set right, and the historical margin separating individuals, ethnic groups, tribes, nations, races are overcome and transcended in Jesus' teaching. Thus, *khankho* is the gospel message of the Kuki people even before the name 'Jesus' was heard.[59]

4.5. Communitarian Value System of the Kuki People

There are certain communitarian values in the Kuki culture which are either died out or hardly exist in some form due to the onslaught of greed culture of western individualism, capitalism, cyber culture etc. these forces together adversely affect the youths of the present age resulting to idleness, lethargy and selfish motif etc. Hence, it is important to re-look at the communitarian values practiced among the youths in earlier days so as to re-inculcate and revive for its theological significance today.

4.5.1. *Lom/Lawm*[60] as the Kuki Youth Organizational Set-Up

Before getting started on *Lom* as communitarian value, let's try to understand the definition given by Thanzauva, "Communitarianism is a concept and life principle of tribal community in which a

[56] Hemkhochon Chongloi, "Khankhology...," 95.

[57] Matt.5:23-24.

[58] Psalm 133:1-3.

[59] Hemkhochon Chongloi, "Khankhology...," 96.

[60] *Lom/Lawm* – as there is no unanimity with regard to literature among the Thadou Kukis, spellings differs from writer to writer. Therefore, the spelling is interchangeably used. In this case, the researcher prefers to use *lom*.

homogenous people live together sharing their joy and sorrows in mutual love and care."[61] To be truly human requires as being in communion with other and living in community is not the same as living in society.[62] Communitarianism cannot be discarded as a primitive philosophy of life irrelevant for modern society. Rather it is intrinsic to human nature and essential for human beings to be truly human[63] and vigorous component for the renewal of the society. There is a sense of security among the members in the community, as the entire widow, the sick and handicapped are taken care of by the community. Being in community, they build their houses together, labour together in their *jhum,* mourn and celebrate together.[64] Such was the same value shared among the Kuki youths in and through the social organization of *Lom.*[65] The members of *Lom* used to work in each other's field in rotational basis regardless of the capability of each individual. It was a collective service aimed at developing a sense of responsibility among the youth.[66] Its origin and development of *Lom* is accredited to the Chief of the village.[67] To delineate *lom* in descending order, there are *lompi* (senior group), *lom-lai* (junior group), *lom-changpah* (learner or errand group).[68] In the practice of *lom, lom-upa* as the leader of the main functionary maintained discipline among the members; *lom* also served as the training centre for the youths to learn methods of cultivating, acquire the habits of charity so as to extend help to the needy, the destitute and widows

---

[61] K. Thanzauva, *Theology of Community*, 106.

[62] K. Thanzauva, *Theology of Community*, 106.

[63] K. Thanzauva, *Theology of Community*, 109.

[64] K. Thanzauva, *Theology of Community*, 113.

[65] *Lom/Lawm* is another important Kuki social organization. Lom is a Kuki dialect, literally means 'team work' or 'corporate work.' Lom is comprised of Kuki youth, both male and female members of each household in the village.

[66] P. S. Haokip, *Zale'n Gam: The Kuki Nation* (n.p.: Kuki National Organization, 2008), 78.

[67] Tarun Goswami, *Kuki Life and Lore*, 95.

[68] Priyadarshini M. Gangte, "Kuki Chieftainship Through Customary Laws-Its Modern Conceptuality," A Paper Presentation on the eve of The 1st Two-Day Seminar on The Kuki Society: Past, Present & Future, Sielmat Christian College, Lamka (19th & 20th Feb. 2010), 2.

in the village. *Lom* also has its *lom upa* (elderly man) who guides the youths and teaches the art of farming and cultivation of land.[69] The main objective of *lom* was to bring economic development in the village by working together in the fields on a rotational basis.[70] Closely related to *Lom* is a social institution of *Som* which is another important feature of social component that needs to be discussed thoroughly here below.

4.5.2. Social Institution of *Som/Sawm* (village-dormitory)

Som is a Kuki term for institution of learning and bachelors' dormitory that was normally set up in a household. It was an active and effective institution for the Kuki youth where the mode of instruction largely was the oral tradition.[71] Similar to *som* is *Zawlbuk* for Mizos, and *Morung* for the Nagas, *Nokpangtes* or *Dekachang* for the Garo, etc.[72] A group of youths lodging at the lass' house (*somnu-in*) in the night are called as *som*. Traditionally, in this practice there is *som-upa* (elderly man) and *somnu* (lass). This *som-upa* usually teaches handicraft-works to his *som*-mates, while *somnu* on the one hand does some mending and cleaning clothes of the *som*-youths and would arrange cots for their sleep. In reciprocation the *som*-youths also make for her a basket, handicrafts,[73] splitting of cane to make strings called *naang,* and collecting building materials from the forest. Politically, the institution of *som* was the backbone of the village; militarily, it was the defense force and standing army, and educationally, it was the centre for learning discipline, moral and psychological training and social virtues.[74] In similar vein, Thanzauva states that apart from head-hunting and inter-village feuds, the village life was often endangered by the constant attack of

[69] Henkhovum Haolai, *Assam Gama Kukite Thusim*, 51.

[70] P. S. Haokip, *Zale'n Gam: The Kuki Nation,* 79.

[71] P. S. Haokip, *Zale'n Gam: The Kuki Nation,* 77.

[72] K. Thanzauva, "Theology of Zawlbuk," in *Towards a Tribal Theology: the Mizo Perspective*, edited by K. Thanzauva (Jorhat: Mizo Theological Conference, 1989), 99.

[73] Henkhovum Haolai, *Assam Gama Kukite Thusim*, 51-52.

[74] P. S. Haokip, *Zale'n Gam: The Kuki Nation,* 77.

the ferocious wild animals upon the domestic animals and human being as well. Therefore, it was out of compulsion that they had to establish an institution of *Zawlbuk* as to ensure security and peace of the village.[75] However, *som*-institution of the Kuki was more of social concern where every individual rendered their service in any given situation liberally, it came to an end with the emergence of Christianity.[76] *Som/Zawlbuk* came to an end with the emergence of British administration and Christian church.[77]

To some extent *Som-in* and *Zawlbuk* have some commonalities except for some few points: unlike *Zawlbuk, Som-in* did not have any particular house mainly erected for its members rather *Som-in* is referred to a place where *som-nu* (lass) resides. Members of *Som* used to lodge at night in an already existing house; the need for making another *som*-house does not arise. Unlike *Zawlbuk* that did not consist of women folk, *Som* was rather performed in a place wherever there were unmarried lasses, in such a case, *Som* is more inclusive than *Zawlbuk* in its outlook and practices. Thus, Thanzauva has rightly observed that the text (Bible) must be integrated with the context with all its social, economic and political issues that integration should be a hermeneutical fusion of horizons, as the New Testament itself is an integration of Judaism, Greek philosophy and the teaching of Jesus Christ.[78] Thus, looking from a synthetic perspective of Christian faith it has immense capacity to enhance Kuki Christian ecclesiological status.

4.5.3. Theological Significance of *Lom, Som/Zawlbuk*

While on the other hand *Zalwbuk* of the Mizos, Thanzauva affirms that it is the forerunner of the Christian church, therefore, ecclesiology in Mizoram should not be simply imported from the west, rather authentic ecclesiology should emerge out of fusion of

[75] K. Thanzauva, "Theology of Zawlbuk," 100.

[76] A personal interview with Pu Jamkholun Kipgen, village council member on (7th Feb. 2012) , age 72, Sirhima village, Dist. Dimapur Nagaland,

[77] K. Thanzauva, "Theology of Zawlbuk," 103.

[78] K. Thanzauva, "Theology of Zawlbuk," 107.

the concepts of *Zawlbuk* and the Church.[79] *Zawlbuk* has its own limit and vitality if compared with the church. Unlike *Zawlbuk,* the church is more inclusive in its membership irrespective of genders. On the other hand, *Zalwbuk* is concerned with the total welfare and security of the community; it is powerful institution which controls the whole community.[80] However, a) the universal nature of the Church with its mission and membership may be incorporated into the *Zawlbuk*'s exclusivistic nature and mission limited to one village. b) Mission of the church with its one sided focus on spiritual life can adopt *Zawlbuk*'s concern for the total welfare and development of the community. c) The fellowship of *Zawlbuk* is a true *koinonia* which the Church is longing for; it is a fellowship of openness to heart and identification. It is beyond getting together but sharing of problems and joy. This should be continued and adopted in the Christian Church today to remove a formal and stereotype fellowship. d) The continuing process of dialogue, reconciliation and unity found in the *Zawlbuk* should be continued in the Christian Church as to overcome division.[81]

Similarly, although *Lom* and *Som* do not have any particular house as such for gathering like that of *Zawlbuk,* yet these *Lom* and Som aimed at developing a sense of responsibility among the youth, served as the training centre for the youths to learn methods of cultivating, acquire the habits of charity so as to extend help to the needy, the destitute and widows in the village. This *lom,* even in today's context, can be practiced in different forms as to serve and meet different needs. It is this kind of value system that needs to be promoted in the society and Church today as they have immense capacity to safeguard the youths from being victims of globalization and modernization such as money culture, cyber culture, individualistic culture etc. so that *Lom* and *Som* spirited ideals may be continued by blending with Christian spirit. In the very act and practice of *Lom* and *Som*, there is much trust towards one another;

[79] K. Thanzauva, "Theology of Zawlbuk," 106.

[80] Khuanga, "The Role of Christianity in the Socio-Economic Praxis of Mizoram," in *Towards a Tribal Theology*, 5.

[81] K. Thanzauva, "Theology of Zawlbuk," 105-107.

each member is obliged and responsible to fulfil what is due of others. In the 21st century the *Som* or *Lom* of the same shapes and forms may not be necessarily applicable in every context yet it can be practiced in different forms. For example, the practice of money-tender on the monthly basis could be considered as a replacement for *lom,* in which act, members are enabled to obtain some desirable goods for their household. Rendering philanthropic service in the realms of education—giving free tuition to the needy students; banking and loan—bankers can devote their services to the denizens/villagers in terms of availing loan and other related opportunities. There are number of ways where persons in higher occupations can contribute for the growth of the communities without any egocentric motifs and selfish gains by adopting *khankho* way or method.

4.6. The Tribal Philosophical Foundation

The tribal philosophy, wisdom, knowledge about Supreme Being, gods and goddesses, myth/folktales, religious beliefs etc. are drawn from the space/land. Hence, space or land becomes a key to liberation and a point of departure[82] for doing indigenous Christian theology. Everything is inter-connected.

4.6.1. The Land and Its People

The primal Kuki and other tribal understanding of land is based on communitarian value system, even human being a part from land cannot be understood, and cannot be treated as separate entity. Whether it is chieftainship or non-chieftainship system of land, the structure of land relationships among the tribals have been communitarian in nature. Besides the Kukis, several tribes such as the Konyaks, Semas, Khasis, Mizos etc. come under chieftainship.[83] In the context of the Kuki, the chief has absolute right of ownership over the entire land of the village. The villagers have no right over the land whatsoever.[84] However, in true sense of the term, his rule was/is not exploitative nor can it be equated with Indian

[82] A. Wati Longchar, *An Emerging Asian*, 8.

[83] A. Wati Longchar, *The Tribal Religious,* 104.

[84] Priyadarshini M. Gangte, "Evolution of the ...," 1.

zamindar system. The Kuki chief has the legitimate authority over the villagers. The chief distribute to every household a plot of land, assisted by his 'Semang-Pachong' (Ministers-MLAs).[85] The chief, howsoever absolute his right over the land but normally carries out in consultation with his council of ministers owing to the land cultivate and utilize as per their requirements of each household.[86] In the Kuki primal tradition, even in *jhum* cultivation certain agricultural rituals were performed as to propitiate and acknowledge the ownership of the land to evil spirits called 'Gampi/Gampipa.'[87] L. Seilen pointed out that the Kukis of ancient time although agreed *Chung Pathen* as creator and owner of everything, yet their understanding of Supreme Being as owner and creator was more theoretical than practical as they were easily overshadowed by the spirits out of fear thus, leading to placation and propitiation which is obvious in their consultation of the spirits to ascertain whether the chosen site for *jhum* cultivation would be acceptable, profitable and allowed.[88] Whatever disruption occurred they understood the spirits as keepers or stewards of the land.[89] As such no random exploitation and commercialization were heard of but land cultivation used to be carried out as a community, as earmarked by the village chief and his council of ministers.

Various festivals of the Kukis are also not without relating to glorifying of land. The festivals are primarily about thanksgiving and dedication to *Pathen* or Supreme God. Some of the main thanksgiving festivals are *Chang Kut* (paddy), *Mim Kut* (Job's tear), *Pawl Kut* (general harvest), *Chapphou/Chapchar Kut* (in preparation for jhum or swidden cultivation, which involves clearing of the land by slash and burn method), *Lom Sel Neh* (a celebration by young people after the season's work is done) and *Hun* or *Ahkangtha* (celebrated after planting of grains and vegetables, an occasion of

---

[85] George T. Haokip, "Change in Kuki's Traditional Land System: A Review," A Paper, 1.

[86] Priyadarshini M. Gangte, "Evolution of the Kuki Chieftainship…," 3.

[87] T. S. Gangte, *The Kukis of Manipur,* 192.

[88] L. Seilen, "Ecology and Primal Vision," in *An Emerging Tribal Theology from Kuki,* 111.

[89] L. Seilen, "Ecology and Primal Vision," 113.

worship in which a white rooster is sacrificed without breaking any of its bones). The other two important youth festivals were *Som Kivah* and *Lom* or *Lawm Kivah.*[90] Thus, every festival is directly related to earth from which all sources come. Wait Longchar observes that the observations of the festivals and religious ceremonies are not only for eating, drinking, and merry-making, but are deeply connected with the soil. These are carried out as to invoke Supreme Being's blessing on the soil so that the land may be fertile as they sow. The tribals cannot think of the Supreme Being or the community without relating to land.[91]

4.6.2. The Religious Concepts of the Kukis

In the Kuki primal religious tradition, Supreme Being is conceived in relation to land. The mythical incantations of priest during various occasions verify that there is an understanding of God and gods in the Kuki primal religion. The belief that there is one supreme God unto whom 'Chung Pathen' is addressed in the mythical incantations who lives beyond the visible firmament and to the other gods unto whom 'Nungjai Pathen' is addressed as to mean smaller gods who rule the visible firmament and the world, and are associated with daily activities of humankind. These gods either bless or harm people. This was the reason behind the concept of sacrificing and appeasing the smaller gods came out of this belief.[92] Whereas, the concept of *Chung Pathen* or the source of 'All Creations,' is considered the highest benevolent who lives in heaven, also is omnipotent and omniscient, does not need propitiation.[93] Literally, Pathen is a combination of two words or syllables: *Pa* (Father), *Then* (Holy), and *chung* (above)

---

[90] Som/Lom Kivah: the young men would find out the longest, straightest and biggest wild bamboo available and erect it at a central place where the Lom festival would be held. Festival time was a break from months of hard work for the village youths. They would compete in various sports, such as wrestling, pestle-throw; high jump over a mithun/bison.

[91] A. Wati Longchar, *The Tribal Religious Tradition*, 119.

[92] Satkhokai Chongloi, "The Unseen Christ of the Kuki People," in *An Emerging Tribal Theology*, 144.

[93] T. S. Gangte, *The Kukis of Manipur*, 161.

is an adjective of *Pathen*—"Holy Father Above."[94] There is another God called *Noimangpa* literally means 'one who rules the world.' The name *Noimangpa* is uttered in incantation in connection with the digging of hole/earth on ritualistic occasions. Digging of the soil involved a dialogue between *Pathen* and *Noimangpa* enacted by the priest regarding who should grant permission for such human's action. In the origin of myth, Chongthu and party emerged from the underworld region ruled by *Noimangpa* who is made in charge of affairs below but ultimately *Pathen* grants permission. Every prayer offered by the priest *Noimangpa* is paired with *Chung Pathen*.[95] According to A. Wati Longchar, for the tribals, the affirmation that "the Supreme Being created the land and it belongs to God" is the starting point of theology. The land is the centre and key for understanding the tribal worldview. Human selfhood, the Supreme Being, the Spirit, history and ethics are defined and perceived only in relation to the land. In short, the land is the basic component of the spirituality of the tribal people.[96] The tribal myths and rhetoric speak of the land as belonging to the Supreme Being. Although, human's ownership of land is claimed in its narrower sense but within the wider understanding and greater recognition, the land belongs to the Supreme Being because the whole land is the home of the Supreme Being.[97] In the tribal views, the land and the Supreme Being are inseparably related. The Supreme Being indwells not only in human persons but also in creation. This interrelatedness of land-Supreme Being does not mean tribal religion as pantheistic as there is no evidence that the tribal myths speak of Supreme Being to be everything, and everything to be the Supreme Being. Rather Supreme Being is manifested in the natural objects and phenomena.[98] The tribal religion does not have a written sacred scripture like other religions, the land and the people

---

[94] M. Thongkhosei Haokip, *Ecumenism,* 35.

[95] Hemkhochon Chongloi, *Indoi,* 136-137.

[96] A. Wati Longchar, "Dancing with the Land: Significance of Land for Doing Tribal Theology," in *Doing Theology with Tribal Resources; Context and Perspective*, edited by A.Wati Longchar and Larry E. Davis (Jorhat: Tribal Study Centre, 199), 118.

[97] Wati Longchar, "Dancing with the Land...," 118-119.

[98] Wati Longchar, "Dancing with the Land...," 119.

themselves are the living sacred scripture.[99] In this sense, the cultural-religious practices that helped them and their surroundings can be deemed as the unwritten Scriptures of the tribals. K. Thanzauva observes that for tribals land is the source of life and is sacred, for there is no other temple except the land itself. Land is the gift of God, who at the same time, dwells in the land. Land owns the tribal community and gives them their identity. Thus, land is integral to their concept of history.[100] The Supreme Being not only indwells in human persons but also in creation. Thus, the land is life. The land is the symbol of unity, personhood and identity. The tribals believe that the Earth is the Mother of all, through earth ancestors' origin are traced, earth is the provider of the needs, giver of life, a dwelling place of spirits, gods and goddesses.[101]

The Kukis also believed in the existence of other powers and beings such as *Nungzai* or *Lungzai* etc. Some considered *Nungzai* as the wife of *Pathen*, while others held it as an independent deity. But due to the malevolent in nature, it is considered as the source of all evils and misfortune. Therefore, people had to do sacrificial offerings for appeasement.[102] The Kukis also believed in the existence of spirits and demons. There are three types of spirits: (a) *Thingbul ngah*—the spirits of forests (b) *Songbul ngah*—the spirits of rocks and stones and (c) *Twi khum ngah*—the spirits of streams of *Twi Khum* is king. The Kukis also believed in the existence of benevolent and malevolent spirits. The former spirit is thought to be responsible for the welfare and prosperity of humans, whereas, the latter spirit is dangerous and destructive to humans. Benevolent spirits are *Chomnu* (short lady), *Lhangnel* (fair water fairy), *Pheisam* or *Maltong* (mutilated leg)—one who gives riches, *Lhadam* (ghost of the dead who is supposed to console the bereaved families). Malevolent spirits are *Gamhoise* (horrid demon), *Kaose* (a demon who is believed to enter a person and cause havoc), *Lhomi* (spirit that can turn to men

---

[99] Wati Longchar, "Dancing with the Land…," 119-120.

[100] K. Thanzauva, *Theology of Community*, 173.

[101] Hrangthan Chhungi, "Heritage of the Tribal Religious Practices in India: An Ecological Concern," in *Theologizing Tribal Heritage*, 158.

[102] M. Thongkhosei Haokip, *Ecumenism*, 36.

or animal), *Zoumi sang* (a tall female spectre). They also believed in some peculiar objects that are said to have supernatural powers such as *Mana*, *Fetish* and *Totem*. *Mana* is a supernatural power infused in any object such as a peculiar stone, tree, plant, humans and animals. *Indoi* (house magic) is one such instance of *Mana*. Fetish is believed to be inhibited by a spirit and thus supposed to confer its power upon the person who possesses it—*Salung*,[103] *Changlung*,[104] etc. are such instances of *Fetish*. Totem is a natural object or an animate being such as animal, bird or insect that is very closely related to a group and in that group of people is believed to descend from the animal or any of the species. Hence according to the Thadous, *Mithun* is considered their mythological ancestor, and python is totem for Chongthu clan. [105]

The Kukis also believed in ancestor worship and the continuity of human soul after death, omens and divinations, dreams etc. Their deceased ancestor spirit is believed to be present among the family, comforting and blessing them because they believed that the deceased spirit of their ancestor exists for a long period. In Kuki religion or *Sakho*, nature plays a vital role; they observe omens meticulously before anything was undertaken that are related to work, journey, farming, hunting, war, etc. they also practiced divination (foretelling) that predicts the future with supernatural aid. Some common practices of divination are by cock, bamboo, egg, rice, etc. these practices are indicative of how nature plays a vigorous role in Kuki *Sakho*.[106]

4.6.3. Theological Significance of Land

The tribal world view challenges us to view land in the context of God-world-human relationships: a) It challenges us to see God as integral part of creation, God suffers when creation suffers. b) It challenges us to see the incarnate Jesus organically related to the total eco-system. c) It challenges us to see the work of the Holy Spirit in

---

[103] A person who has this *salung* can kill animals easily.

[104] A person who has this *salung* will have a bountiful harvest.

[105] M. Thongkhosei Haokip, *Ecumenism*, 36-37.

[106] M. Thongkhosei Haokip, *Ecumenism*, 38.

a wider perspective. d) The space-centered theology challenges us to see salvation in holistic perspective. e) A space-centered theology challenges us to see ourselves as an integral part of the macro-organism and f) It demands us a radical change of attitude towards natural resources.[107] James H. Cone asserts that "What people think about God, Jesus Christ, and the Church cannot be separated from their own social and political status in a given society."[108] It is also true for the tribal people that their culture, religion and spirituality cannot be separated from "creation/land" or "space." Human always understand themselves as an integral part of creation/land and not apart from it. Land/space is the foundational theology of self-understanding out of which liberation, justice, and then peace will flow naturally and necessarily. Therefore, justice to creation/land is the key to liberation and human dignity. Thus, harmony with "space" is the starting point of the tribal people's spirituality and their search for liberation from the dominant theologies and from inferiority complex.[109] On the contrary, sadly, due to the onslaught of the modernization with its market culture and Europeanized Christianity in the tribal regions, especially in the Kuki regions, people start seeing lands as profiteering assets. Hence, everyone would witness the consequences; there is an adulteration in terms of commercializing the mother-earth. Although, earth being personified as mother, the sanctity of a mother-earth is lost or a motherhood identity is adulterated resulting to loss of vast lands within the community and it is beyond reparable.

The anthropocentric tradition of Christian theology has been largely responsible exclusive understanding of God's care for all the creations. Hung Po Ho has rightly argued about this in his book *Embracing the Household of God* that states;

> ...the theological foundation of Christian religion is Triune God as creator of the universe, its doctrine of soteriology, which is based on the incarnation, crucifixion and resurrection of Jesus Christ, the God-man figure,

[107] A. Wati Longchar, *An Emerging Asian Theology*, 89-91.

[108] James H. Cone, *God of the Oppressed* (New York: Orbis Books, 1997) , 41.

[109] A. Wati Longchar, *An Emerging Asian Tribal Theology: Issue, Method and Perspective* (Jorhat: Tribal Study Centre, Eastern Theological College, 2000), 25-26.

> perceived through the Jewish historical background and in the context of the early church, has been directed exclusively towards the human species. The doctrinal arguments regarding sin, salvation (redemption), and consummation (kingdom of God, heaven and hell) are all overwhelmingly concentrated on human destiny.[110]

He goes on pointing out that "The first ecumenical council in Nicaea was convened by Roman Emperor Constantine, for the purpose of solidifying his empire through the unity of bishops and churches. The creed produced by this council, thus focused on the most divisive issue among the early church bishops, i.e., Christology." The same has been observed by S. J Samartha "When the council of Nicaea met, presided over by Emperor Constantine, who at that time was an unbaptized Christians, (he was baptized only in 337 A.D. the year he died), political considerations were mixed up with matters of doctrine."[111] So, for the purpose of solidifying his empire through the unity of bishops and churches the Nicaean council was called by the Emperor Constantine. Therefore the whole doctrinal arguments on Christology were overwhelmingly concentrated on human destination alone such as sin, salvation, consummation (heaven or hell) at the expense of creation-culture.

Within this anthropocentric theological framework, further consequences had taken place in the Christian world of Europe, which is aptly evidenced by Max Weber (1864-1920), a German religious sociologist and political economist, that states;

> ...ascetic Protestantism was one of the major "elective affinities" that determined the rise of capitalism. In his book, *The Protestant Ethics and the Spirit of Capitalism* Weber observes that the Protestant ethic proposed by John Calvin induced people to engage enthusiastically in work in the secular world, causing them to develop business

---

[110] Huang Po Ho, *Embracing the Household of God: A Paradigm Shift from Anthropocentric Tradition to Creation Responsibility in Doing Theology*, (Kolkota: PTCA, 2014), 21.

[111] S. J. Samartha, *One Christ—Many Religions*, 141.

> enterprises, to engage in trade and eventually to accumulate wealth for investment. He concluded that the Protestant ethic was a force behind an unplanned, uncoordinated mass action that influenced the development of capitalism.[112]

Although hard work is part of human virtue however, this trait, without proper plan, when connected to capitalist habit of accumulating wealth ultimately resulted negatively thus leading to egocentrism, greed, market competition, materialism and ecological exploitation. This has further impacted particularly, upon the tribal cultures and generally, across the globe.

4.6.4. Myth as Theological Foundation

Some modern people like Benedict Spinoza and Thomas Hobbes considered myth as erroneous interpretation of nature, due to faulty reasoning. On the contrary, another German classical scholar Christian Gottlob Heyne defined myth as language by which primitive people described their inner states and reacted to their environment. Thus, he conceives myth as the fertile womb out of which eventually historiography, religion, philosophy, poetry and literature proceed.[113] Similarly, Mircea Eliade echoes, myth for primitive and archaic societies was the very foundation of social life and culture as such the myth is thought to express the absolute truth, because it narrates a sacred history, i.e. trans-human revelation which took place at the dawn of Great Time, in the holy time of the beginning.[114] Hence, myth can be taken as a worldview by which the tribals perceive divine knowledge, supernatural etc. Like the Ancient Near-East creation stories as found in the Bible, the Kuki or the Chongthus, the progenitor of the Thadou Kukis, have their own

---

[112] Huang Po Ho, *Embracing the Household of God: A Paradigm Shift from Anthropocentric Tradition to Creation Responsibility in Doing Theology*, (Kolkota: PTCA, 2014), 19-20.

[113] J.D. Douglas, et al., *New 20th Century Encyclopaedia of Religious Knowledge*, second edition (Michigan: Baker Book House, 1991), 582.

[114] Mircea Eliade, "Myths, Dreams, and Mysteries: The Encounter between Contemporary Faiths and Archaic Realities," in *Theological Collections: Myth and Symbol*, edited by. F. W. Dillistone (London: SPCK, 1966), 35.

mythical stories that attempt to explain the heavens, creation and the world. The origin of the creation by *Pathen* is extracted from the incantation by the priest during worship for curing ailments caused by the water which says:

> *Pathen* created heaven and earth. He created all types of trees and water. You (water) went down into *heilhuongpi* (oceans) which was seven strata below the surface of the earth. You then appeared through the roots of the banana and the *thelpi* (a kind of plants having broad leaves often used in packing of salts, etc. in the tribal bazaar).[115]

Pathen is also the creator of god called *Nungjai* and two more spirits called *Vansum* and *Vanleng*. During all the ritualistic rites for purification of the evil spirits the priest at the beginning of the rituals invariably offers drops of wine to propitiate the almighty God and his assistant, the god *Nungjai*.[116] Furthermore, a mythical story of how the earth came into being is narrated:

> *Pathen* created the earth called *Leiset*. The surface of the earth was a huge mass of stony crust void of soil. This happened due to the ejection of soil by the stars in the form of their excreta into the bottom of the earth called *Noijum*. Two earth-worms called *Chalpinu* and *Chalpipa* who were living in the bottom of the earth had eaten up the falling excreta. These two worms ultimately defecated the soily excreta on the stony crust. Thus soil originated on the surface of the earth in the form of mountains, hills, valleys and dales.[117]

Song has rightly observed in this regard that there is no community that does not have myth or stories of how the world came into being. Although, Song's conviction rests upon the unscientific account of how the universe came into being, yet he denies an

---

[115] Tarun Goswami, *Kuki Life and Lore*, 212.

[116] Tarun Goswami, *Kuki Life and Lore*, 212

[117] Tarun Goswami, *Kuki Life and Lore*, 213.

illusionary tale of an irrational mind.[118] In similar vein, the myth of creation found in the Kuki legends may equally lack any scientific account yet they cannot merely be reduced to illusionary tale of the past because a kind of intuition involves by which people understand the creation of the world and human beings. Myths are created to protect life – it is the foundation of tribal worldview. Even the two creation accounts of the Genesis, which is not without the influence of Ancient Near East epics, fall neither in the category of ahistorical nor historical, nor are they considered mythical, legendary alike but it is a gist of information of how the world came into existence in a form of 'report.' This is a well-accepted theory among the biblical scholars. However, in the end, what matters most is not 'how' or 'where' or 'when' but what message it conveys to the recipients for their life foundation and spiritual renewal is most important.

There are numerous legendary tales of the Kuki heroes and heroines that may not be totally reduced to mythical characters such as *Galngam/Rhalngam* and *Hangsai, Khupting* and *Ngambom, Pujil* and *Langchal, Benglam, Jonlhing* and *Nanglhun, Chemtatpa/Temtatpa, Changkhatpu* and *Ahsijolneng, Khalvompu* and *Lenchanghoi* have entertained many generations[119] yet these mythical stories are not without its place and names. So, in that sense, merely reducing to purely mythical could be fatal blunder. Rather one should be able to recognize the historical weights of its mythical stories. Some of these mythical stories may be theologically treated in the succeeding chapter. One folktale *Benglam* Kuki can be further narrated which can be related in the context of ecological crisis who committed a self-destruction on an ecological tree in the primordial time.

> Once *Benglam* Kuki climbed upon a tree and seated on a branch. He started cutting the base of the branch on which he was sitting. As the branch fell down to the ground, he too fell down along with the branch. He was lying on the ground half dead. In order to ascertain whether he had

[118] C. S. Song, "In the Beginning were Stories, not Texts," in *Theologies and Cultures: Contextual Theologies in Taiwan: An Overview* (June 2008), 10.

[119] P. S. Haokip, *Zale'n Gam: The Kuki Nation*, 84.

died or not he held his ears to know whether they are cold or warm. They were still warm and he was still alive.[120]

The folktale is deemed one of the idiotic and ludicrous of legendary *Benglam*. He was cutting a branch of the tree on which he was sitting, and this 'act of cutting' picturises how foolish he was as it was a suicidal act. In the same vein, though *Benglam* may be jeered at his action by those who heard about him, yet ecologically speaking, human beings at present era are not wiser than him as humans are partly involved in destroying the environment, destroying environment means destroying ourselves, it is slow process of suicide.[121] In this matter Bishop A. S. Hemron rightly asserts that folktales are not just entertaining but had ethical and moral bindings. Folktales are often 'humanized' and made to interact with one another.[122] Thus, folktales are meant for drawing out moral and spiritual vitality which still bear implication for the people today. Our Asian Christian theology should be a drive towards humanization and spiritual fervour to impact our civilization to be more humane. In that sense of need, myth as a humanizing element can be vital for bridging the gap between globalization and the biblical truths.

4.6.4.1. Theological Significance of Myth

T. Vanlaltlani asserts that myths are the ground of religion and culture because they contain religious truth for religious community and its concerned culture and society.[123] Longchar also asserts that Supreme Being works and reveals his/her mysteries through creation. Thus, myth is the sacred "scripture" and "creed" for the tribals.[124] He further holds that myth envisages a holistic view of life; everything is interrelated, interconnected and interdependent.

---

[120] L. Seilen, "Ecology and Primal Vision:...," 109.

[121] L. Seilen, "Ecology and Primal Vision:...," 109.

[122] A. S. Hemron, "Adivasis/Tribal Heritage," in *Theologizing Tribal Heritage: A Critical Re-Look*, edited by Hrangthan Chhungi (Delhi: CWM/ISET-ECC/PCI/ ISPCK, 2008), 134.

[123] T. Vanlaltlani, "Socio-Cultural Heritage of the Tribal People in India North East India Context," in *Theologizing Tribal Heritage*, 90.

[124] A.Wati Longchar, *An Emerging Asian*, 68-69.

Supreme Being, spirits and all creatures are mutually affecting each other. All participate in decision making.[125] T. Vanlaltlani opines that even the highest philosophy of Mizo social and moral life principle called *Tlawmngaihna*[126] (*tomngain*a in Kuki) might have come out of myth with its implication of service without an expectation of any reward.[127] Such social implication of *tomngaina* is seen to have declined to a great extent in the Kuki society today. Therefore, myths of the Kukis are pressing need to the contemporary tribal people.

4.7. A Shift from Tradition to Modernity

Modernization or westernization with all its contemporary culture and technology is the primary cause for detribalization, stripping off the inherited traditions, fashions and mannerism of the tribals. This detribalization promotes anti-tribal ethos, denunciating its social moral and its ethical elements and considered these tribal heritages as things of the past and irrelevant in modern context.[128] With the adoption of western culture, the indigenous people hardly appreciate their own culture; the more they emerge into western mode of life the more their cultural value systems are depreciated. According to George T. Haokip, the Kuki traditional land system, the present era of urbanization and globalization have affected various untouched culture and brought them into interaction with dominant culture. The advent of British colonial rule with its new administration in the hill areas and the spread of democratic ideas and institution in the post-independence on the other hand have largely undergone changes in the practice of traditional land ownership and land system.[129] With the adoption of modernity there was a sudden break, a shift from tradition to modernity, nomadic to settled life creating a situation

---

[125] A.Wati Longchar, *An Emerging Asian*, 72.

[126] *Tlawmngaihna* as explicated by P.L. Lianzuala implies various meanings, it means self-sacrificing, unselfish, self-denying, persevering compared to Hindu term *Niskama Karma* and the Christian love. Cf. P.L. Lianzuala, 'Towards a Theology of Mizo Tlawmngaihna," in *Towards a Tribal Theology: the Mizo Perspective*, edited by K. Thanzauva (Mizo Theological Conference, 1989), 54.

[127] T. Vanlaltlani, "Socio-Cultural Heritage...," 84.

[128] Vanlalchhuanawma, "Keynote Address," 13-14.

[129] George T. Haokip, "Change in Kuki's ...," 2.

of dependency in the fields of technical, business and engineering. Moreover the migrant with superior skills in the pattern of work gets better opportunity which for the tribals was incompatible with their subsistence of slash-and-burn shifting cultivation. As a result, independent economic system of tribals has largely been reduced to a condition of dependency. Some few elites enjoy the wealth and power but majority becomes victims of the new economic system.[130] Even within the Kuki community itself, the powerful section of elite household, other than the Kukis, have encroached the lands of the Kukis thus, affecting the traditional egalitarian society. The land that was considered in the past as asset of 'power' and 'status,' has now changed into money economy and commodity. National Rural Employment Generation Scheme (NREGS) is another factor that heightens up exploitation of land where many new villages have been registered to benefit the scheme which is safe vault to earn a profitable income when the registered villages do not actually exist. The modern administrative system owes its emergence of privatization of land that leads to its co-modification, resulting in mortgaging and sale of land. This creates classes and introduces differentiation and land alienation.[131] True to it, selling of land, terrace field in the village level has been rampant in some Kuki inhabited villages, hence adversely disrupting the smooth functioning of the chieftainship administration.[132] The adoption of modernity also has negative impact in many aspects of life—youth unemployment, dropped-out students and this has furthered to inter-tribal clashes by adopting gun culture as an expression of frustration and revenge in the midst of poverty.[133] Combined factors of Westernized Christianity and modernized culture with its technological competences have largely turned downed the tribal spirituality. Wati Longchar, in this regard, confirms that God has bestowed upon indigenous people a deep

---

[130] A. Wati Longchar, *An Emerging Asian Theology,* 19.

[131] George T. Haokip, "Change in Kuki's...," 4.

[132] Personal interview with Pu Seitinlal Sitlhou, Saijang Village on (8th Feb. 2012), age 35, he is a Social Worker.

[133] S. Thangboi Zou, "The Leibak of Turmoil and Question of Survival," *Ashijolneng* Annual Magazine of Kuki Students' Organisation, (Shillong: Department of Publication Kuki Students' Organisation 11 August, 2007). 74.

spirituality which guides people and teaches them how they must relate to their environment and to each other.[134] Tribal spirituality as expressed by J. Patmury, is the quality of being actively aware of and connected to the reality of the spirit, the one that is beyond or behind its material appearance. Tribal spirituality finds their expression in community rituals. Tribal spirituality comes to best expression during festivals in which the whole tribe is involved.[135] Huang Po Ho also aptly identifies that "Asia as a continent with profound cultures with deep spirituality, there must be elements of Asian spirituality that contains different and distinct form of spirituality."[136] Thus, the spirituality of tribal is overshadowed by the dominant theology. On the contrary, the indigenous tribals are not without their spirituality, the mysterious ability to perceive and relate to their fellow beings, nature and creations are obvious. Therefore, recognizing the spirituality of a particular culture in consonance with the Scriptures should be a point of departure for doing Christian theology in the tribal context that is fulfilling and nourishing.

4.8. Feminist Critique on Land/Creation

Aruna Gnanadason states that it is well established that violence against women is akin to violence against the earth—even words used to describe the two are similar.[137] The body of God wounded due to the present phase of industrialization with its profligate use of the resources of the earth.[138] Eco-feminist theologians have been critical of dominant Christian theology because it has its root in Israelite theology that holds strong patriarchal traditions, male domination and female subordination. Christian theology

---

[134] Wait Longchar, "The Continuity of Indigenous People in Today's World," in *Theologizing Tribal Heritage*, 64.

[135] J. Patmury, "Tribal Spirituality and Christian Mission," in *Christ Among the Tribals*, edited by F. Hrangkhuma & Joy Thomas (Bangalore: Fellowship of Indian Missiologists, 2007), 212-213.

[136] Huang Po Ho, "A Paradigm Shift in Theology: A Holistic Redemption to God's Creation," in *JTCA: The Journal of Theologies and Culture in Asia,* 2 (2012): 83.

[137] Aruna Gnanadason, "Women, Patriarchy and Creation: Insight from Eco-Feminism," in *JTCA,* 58.

[138] Aruna Gnanadason, "Women, Patriarchy...," 60.

takes account of the experience of only men, their understanding about God. Women's understanding and experiencing of God is ignored, regarded as unwise and incapable.[139] Church's sexist and discriminatory language in theology, liturgy and hymns are found discriminative against women. A sexist and discriminatory language is a language in the form of spoken word, images and symbols that are used in exclusion of the other gender of human being, i.e. female folk. Christian theology pictures God as male because it has been shaped and written by men with a male-dominated philosophy and ideology.[140] The image of God the Father, or as a Monarchial Ruler, has led to the hierarchies in Christianity that has given rise not only to androcentrism and a hierarchy in creation, but also to aggressive anthropocentrism.[141] Eco-feminists argue that sexism as the root cause of injustice which leads to war, militarism and rape of the earth. Similarly, in patriarchal society the earth is personified with women. As the earth is referred as female, as mother and so women are also characterized as being more earthly and closer to creation than men who are considered to be rational.[142] Creation/ earth is perceived only to meet the needs and wants of the humanity thereby dominion over it. Against the dominant theological teaching, eco-feminist theologians find out multi-dimensional and complex metaphors for God in the Bible: metaphors such as God as a compassionate, feminine, mothering God who fills the earth with grace and creative power. God is imaged as Shepherd (Ps. 23:1, Matt. 18:10-14); as potter (Jer. 18; 1-6; as mother (Isa. 42:14 and 66:13, Luke 15:8-10). Thus eco-feminists sought out to understand the grace of God through many metaphors; they contend God's intervention in a caring relationship and not in a dominating way.[143] Salie McFague in her book, *The Body of God: An Ecological Theology*, challenges us to remodel our theological attitudes towards other

---

139 R.L. Hnuni, *Vision for Women in India: Perspective from the Bible, Church and Society* (Bangalore: Asian Trading Corporation, 2009), 32-33.

140 R.L. Hnuni, *Vision for Women in India*, 34-35.

141 Aruna Gnanadason, "Women, Patriarchy...," 72.

142 A. Wati Longchar, *An Emerging Asian Theology*, 9.

143 Aruna Gnanadason, "Women, Patriarchy...," 72-73.

creatures. "Humans should not act as namers of and the rulers over creation, but rather act as gardeners, caretakers, parents, stewards, trustees, lovers, priests, co-creators and friends."[144] Eco-feminism challenges us to do away the dualistic view of mind/body, nature/culture, male/female, human/non-human and hierarchy which excludes women. It has opened new way to relate in non-hierarchical and non-patriarchal ways towards culture and creation. Failing to relate in non-hierarchical and non-patriarchal will bring threat to space and injustice against women. Eco-feminism provides us space where men-women and creation create a better and new community for brighter and fuller existence.

4.9. Conclusion

With the advent of Christianity with its modern culture has its adverse effect on Kuki tribal religion and culture in particular and rest of the tribals as a whole. There was a transitional period from tradition to modernity which has in many ways brought different stages of life in the tribal confederation. It was an adoption of western culture and largely a rejection of traditional culture if not a fusion of culture in which many tribals are exposed to confusion. Predominantly there was a decline of communitarian value system, whatever seems tribal or worldview in its outlook is deemed unscientific, backward, irrational, inferior and possessing nothing good. Many philosophical foundations of the tribals such as myths, folktales, folksongs, are discarded. The tribal spirituality was denied to have interaction with biblical stories.

The dominant theology with its anthropocentric and hierarchical view of creation is also largely responsible for ecological crisis and women's subjugation and victimization. This has caused a serious harm upon the tribal land with its motif of dominion over the land. However, having examined all these situations, a shift of theological trend from dominant theology to tribal liberation theology takes place as an encounter.

[144] Wati Longchar, "Ecumenical Responses to Ecological Crisis: A Critique from the Indigenous Peoples' Perspective," in *JTCA: The Journal of Theologies and Cultures in Asia; Green Theology; An Asian Ecumenical Response to Eco-Justice*, 11 (2012): 146.

Chapter 5

A Theological Appraisal on the Kuki Culture from C.S. Song's Theology of Cultures

5.1. Introduction

In this chapter effort is to comprehend the Kuki culture from Song's theology of cultures so as to engender a biblical-cultural interaction. In other words, it is an attempt to understand culture of a particular community for its theological significance in light of Song's theology of cultures. In our theological-cultural enterprise, what is imperative is to make our cultural resources or elements indigenously theological or vice versa so that the gospel presented in Western garb is unmasked and is understood originally in and through the cultural thought form of an indigenous community. Folktales and other legendries have the potentials to expose and understand the mystery of the tribal religio-cultural worldviews of a particular time through the present situation. Their predicaments and triumphal events expressed in the forms of folktales and folksongs exist orally in the community. So, one could unambiguously identify folktales and others alike as gateway to penetrate the worldviews of the tribals. New Testament scholars are unanimous that a parable is, literally, something "cast alongside" something else. Jesus' parables were stories that were cast alongside a truth in order to illustrate that truth. Jesus narrated parables by using a story method. So, Jesus employed an earthly story with a heavenly meaning. Jesus' parables were teaching aids. Hence, story and parables are interrelated employed to disclose mysterious meaning to the hearers. It is a dialogue between the biblical truth and the cultural resources of truths of the Kuki people. Huang Po Ho remarks, "Dialogue is thus, understood as a method not only to be informed and to be enriched with one's own faith tradition through such engagement but is also a path to heal the divisive relations in and between human communities and societies."[1] The Kuki tribal do have numbers of parables, legends and stories that orally exist that are never or hardly meant to have meaningful message in the past or present. Here are some few instances that can be underlined so to create lively inter-cultural dialogue with the biblical truths in our theological-cultural exploration.

5.2. Theological Significance of Mythical Stories

5.2.1. Tale of Benglam

> The Adventures of Benglam is one of the most exciting stories of Kuki folklores in Kuki Zalen'gam (land of freedom) that comprises of the Kuki inhabited northeastern Indian region, Chittagong Hills Track of Bangladesh and the Kangmaiphaicham (Kabaw valley) of Myanmar (Burma). The time when he dies is lost to the realm of history. Historians believed that he was the contemporary of Philo (Greek) and Confucius (Chinese), the antic wise men of the west and the east. He goes by various names such as, the name of Penglam to the Kuki-Chin, and Chhura to the Kuki-Mizo. The people during his days were head-hunters whose might and value was judged from the numbers of head he could collect to do the front wall of his house. One who had

[1] Huang Po Ho, *Embracing*, 81.

taken the highest number of heads is regarded as a great soldier or warrior and placed highly in the power ring of the Village. He is the uncrowned king in the Village. As such, groups of warrior will always patrol their village and will always be on the lookout for their enemies who might have roamed in the forest by himself.

On one such day, Benglam had started out for his Jhum to see his crops. From a distance he could see that a smoke was coming up from his *buk* (small hut), which was in the centre of his field, fearing that his enemies might be the one that made the fire, he hit upon a plan. He called out, "my buk", hello! "My buk," but there was no reply. Then he said "Arre! How is it? What happened to you my buk? Why don't you answer me as you did before?" His enemy, thinking that the *buk* did not answer because of their presence and decided to answer on the *buk's* behalf and called out "Hoi"(Yes) in unison.

As soon as he heard his enemies' voices, he started running away. His enemies pursued him and come to a place where he hid under a big log lying in the corner of the field. The pursuers soon arrived at the spot where he was hiding. One amongst them branding a spear climbed onto the log and spearing the log said, "If Benglam were here, I would have speared him like this and like that." Benglam was very much frightened, crying "Stop! Stop! You would really hurt me," and he came out from his hiding and was immediately caught.

The enemies then discussed how they were to take prisoner home. Benglam, full of wit said, once we caught and led a prisoner by his nose. So, if you held me by my nose, I would not be able to run away. When they started to return home, Benglam pretended that he could not walk fast and within no time they were lagging far behind. Seeing his chance he blew his nose, jerked his head and was free again. The man who led him had his hand full of

> snot. While he was busy cleaning the snot, Benglam made a good escape.
>
> When the warrior called his friends, Benglam was nowhere to be seen. Frustrated and angry, they resumed their search. At lunch hour they took rest under a shady tree and had their food. Benglam who was on that tree observed them and unconsciously spoke out, saying, "Hei! See, the smallest man is taking the biggest bite" (as among them the smallest man bite the biggest bone) and revealed his presence and was caught again.
>
> This time we would not heed your suggestion, said the leader of the party. But all the same, they were very much worried. They did not know how to take a prisoner home alive. Till this time they had only taken home the heads of a warrior they had killed in a fight. At last Benglam again suggested that he should be led the way they had once led a prisoner home by the elbow.
>
> Fearing that he might escape again, the leader of the group took charge of him. When he tied to hold the folded elbow, Benglam hit him (with all his might) on his nose; blood oozed out from his nose and in the confusion that followed, Benglam disappeared from sight and went on his way.
>
> The warriors promised themselves not to breathe a word of the day's incident and did not trouble Benglam again for quite sometimes. Seeing that his adventure with the warrior had ended, he went to seek adventure elsewhere.[2]

A philosophical insight one could observe from this tale is that it is the brain that matters and never the colour of the outward appearance that makes human being a genius and genuine. Benglam depicted wit and wisdom. Although, Benglam's stories exist in oral forms for his comical and hilarious actions in the

---

[2] By James Vaiphei, http://kukiforum.com/2003/09/the-great-escape-of-benglam-legendary-folklore-depicting-wit-and-wisdom/ (28/03/2019)

communities, a closer study of his tales would bring one to a sense of shrewd and prompt response to a given situation. Jesus advises us to be always wise and alert, "See, I am sending you out like sheep into the midst of wolves; so be wise as serpents and innocent as doves."[3] This reminds that one should be careful and mindful of his/her action and the consequences.

5.2.2. Tale of Miss Khupting and Mr. Ngambom

Here is the summary of the duo love story that is so attached to the name of its village, culture of the people, and the time setting called 'Ngambom Khang' or 'Ngambom Era' that no one denies the historicity of the popular love story that is widely narrated within a particular community. However, undoubtedly, at some point it sounds mystical and beyond human comprehension:

> Once upon a time, in one of the Kuki villages located between the present border of Myanmar and Mizoram, there were two female friends each of them married to poor men. After giving birth to one baby girl each, they began to conceive for the next babies in their wombs. Alongside pregnancy, they practiced *lomcha*, (a traditional way of work, one day at one's field and the other day at another's field). One day it so happened that the pain stroke their bellies and to their dismay, the two friends, simply rubbed their bellies, and immediately the pain subsided. The following day, the same panic occurred, and they applied the same technique. Soon this had become a panacea to heal their pain. One day the other friend asked to her friend that if the babies that they were carrying were born, if one was a male child, the other a female child, they should have had them get married. They both agreed and kept all things confidential, even from their spouses.
>
> To their surprise, a baby boy and a baby girl were born to them respectively; the baby boy was named Mr. Ngambom,

[3] Matthew 10:16.

and the other baby girl, Miss Khupting. The babies looked beautiful and bright in their appearance.

After months of rest, they also regained their strength and resumed their field work. Since they had no one at home to take care of their babies, they had to bring their babies to the field. They would lay down their babies upon a separate cradling place (this was done by levelling the slope area of the ground and by putting a branch of wood to support the cradle), Miss Khupting above and Mr. Ngambom beneath. The two mothers worked beside the place where they laid their babies. Whenever they would come for feeding their babies, to their surprise, they would see Mr. Ngambom lying with Miss Khupting, very close to each other. Every day the duo mothers were surprised by the unusual behaviour of their babies.

All through the year, this had become a usual witness of the two mothers. One fateful day, to her curiosity, Miss Khupting's mother put her eye on to the unusual behaviour of Mr. Ngambom. To her utter surprise, she noticed that Mr. Ngambom converted himself into salamander and crawled towards Miss Khupting and laid himself beside Miss Khupting. However, Miss Khupting's mother kept everything to her heart and did not disclose what she had seen to Mr. Ngambom's mother. But she began to develop doubt on Mr. Ngambom's blood linage and his parents. However, she continued her friendship as usual as before until the time their romance came to public arena and became talk of the villagers. By then, Miss Khupting's mother warned her daughter Miss Khupting that she should be cautious of Mr. Ngambom and keep distance from him.

As Mr. Ngambom and Miss Khupting grew, they excelled the youths of their ages in every aspect; Mr. Ngambom had distinctive quality of nobility, heights, courteousness, prowess, sportsmanship, integrity and truthfulness in all his works. Miss Khupting also proved to be the icon of her days. She was ornately beautiful, tall, lovely and excelled others in her musical masterpiece of *Lhemlhei* lyric, known for her hospitality, meekness and skilful in shawl weaving. Their fame grew far and wide. Whenever they played games, everyone wanted to be on their side because of the excellent abilities. As their romance grew deeper and became more public. At times, Mr. Ngambom's parents also felt that it was a perfect time for their son's marriage, Mr. Ngambom's parents also prepared their *tuchas* and *bechas* (customarily they are philosopher and friends) and went them alongside to Miss Khupting's parents to sue their marriage for the first time, and the discourse went on to the extent of disclosing what had they both agreed when the two conceiving babies were in their wombs. But to their surprise, all their efforts resulted unsuccessful. So, seemingly the situation turned out to be impossible for the young lovers to fulfil their long cherished dream of being together for the rest of their lives. The more the girl's parents cautioned and imposed strict vigilance on their daughter, the more they became serious about their love for each other. So, their love accelerated beyond human control and imagination, though impossible from the parents and others' perspective yet at heart they were already one.

After the first attempt shattered them, one afternoon Mr. Ngambom visited his fiancée when nobody else was there, and he asked for a strand of her hair. She gladly accepted her boyfriend's request. After a while Mr. Ngambom left her taking alongside a strand of hair and straight away went to Tieo river. He carved out the image of Miss Khupting from the wax of bees and kept there at the corner of the river. He put her hair in the arrow pouch and kept it airtight. Then, Miss Khupting's health began to deteriorate. Mr. Ngambom executed his magical power by making his fiancée ill in order to do away the stubbornness of Miss Khupting's parents owing to their marriage. As Miss Khupting became very ill, her parents immediately called the local priests and doctors but none could do anything for her health improvement. At last, Miss Khupting's parents, out of no way, made a vow that she should be married to whosoever could make her recovered from her illness. So, Mr. Ngambom, upon hearing what was pronounced, went to Miss Khupting and made her well again through his magic.

Subsequently, Mr. Ngambom's parents made their second attempt for their son's marriage. This time Mr. Ngambom told his parents confidently that they should succeed the fact that Miss Khupting's parents made a vow that they would make their daughter marry to the one who brought complete healing upon her illness. However, to their dismay, their second attempt also went in vain.

The second time Mr. Ngambom went to Tieo river and executed the same magic. Soon, Miss Khupting's health was worse than before. Her parents immediately called the local priests and doctors but only to their hopelessness. Finally, Miss Khupting's parents vowed the same thing as the first instance that they would let their daughter marry to whosoever would bring complete healing over her illness. Even the second time, Mr. Ngambom , through his magical power, brought back Miss Khupting's life. Everyone, young and old celebrated about Miss Khupting's health recovery. This time many people advised Miss Khupting's parents to grant their proposal for marriage but Miss Khupting's parents, especially, her mother stood adamant to their marriage proposal. Rather she became more hostile towards their marriage and vowed poignantly that if she would, at any rate, permit Miss Khupting's marriage to Mr. Ngambom, her throat would become choked.

The third time, Mr. Ngambom went again to Tieo river and executed the same magic. This time Miss Khupting's health was worse than the first two. Miss Khupting's parents immediately called the local priests and doctors but only to their utter dismay, all their efforts went in vain. Before Miss Khupting's parents could call Mr. Ngambom, there was heavy rainfall and storm and the curved image object of Miss Khupting, which Mr. Ngambom used to keep at Tieo river was taken away by the tide of the water. Simultaneously, he ran rushing back and forth along the river to find out where it was but failed to get back the curved image object of Miss Khupting and he thus began to conceive that Miss Khupting, her fiancée, was no more. Mr. Ngambom suddenly cried out aloud and was driven half mad. Nothing could replace his pain and love for her lover Miss Khupting in life. As the village people were trying to bury Miss Khupting's dead body, the coffin kept expanding in size and could not place the coffin into the burial place. The larger they dug the burial ground, over and again, yet the size of the coffin kept expanding in size; hence, this made impossible to bury her dead. Until Mr. Ngambom came and bid farewell to Miss Khupting, they could not bury her. Thereafter, Mr. Ngambom was driven half-mad and tarried his days in the thick forest where nobody else should see him. But his unsolicited behaviour caused his parents a miserable life, his parents had no rest until Mr. Ngambom came back home.

Although, physical parting invaded their lives but their profound love for each other superseded both the physical and spiritual realms. The duo lovers even after living in two different worlds, their profound love occasioned them to meet each other in the spiritual world called *mithikho* or *thikhol khul* with the help of Sangah (wildcat) in which Mr. Ngambom could enter the spiritual realm where Miss Khupting was residing. It so happened that Miss Khupting used to send the wild cat to pluck the flowers that was planted on her graveyard by her boyfriend Mr. Ngambom. Upon noticing by Mr. Ngambom about the plucking of the flowers, and so to his anxiousness to catch the culprit, one night he promptly watched out secretly, and to his amazement, Sangah (wildcat) came and he immediately seized it. Upon interrogating, Sangah revealed that it was Miss Khupting who sent it to pluck the flowers. Then Mr. Ngambom asked Sangah to take him where Miss Khupting was. Although, Sangah disclosed the difficulty and great chasm between the spiritual world and the physical world, yet over his tenacious urge, Sangah at last agreed to go with it where Miss Khupting was. So, tradition says that Sangah helped Mr. Ngambom to pass through many life-threatening path ways; such as an abyss, wild animal kingdom, steep mountains, Kulsamnu (similar to Catholic tradition of purgatory in which Kulsamnu, an ugly woman, she enslaved and tortured the spirits of the wicked and evil people), and vast expanse of oceans. In all these obstacles, Sangah made him passed through till the place where Miss Khupting was. There in the spiritual world, Mr. Ngambom had another chance to meet and spent time with his unforgettable and dearest lover Miss Khupting. There, Mr. Ngambom name changed into Pabom and had funny fishing and hunting experiences with the people of spiritual world. He also built one beautiful house, in which people of the spiritual world (*Mithikho*) were filled with amazement. So, Pabom spent quite sometimes there in *Mithikho*. However, one thing that did not fulfil his desire was that, although he met his sweetheart Miss Khupting in *Mithikho*, Pabom, being in his real physical body, actually could not make any physical contact with her. Tradition says that during night, Miss Khupting was found to be in mere skeletal bones in the eyes of Mr. Ngambom and to his utter ignorance, he would throw it away those bones sideways. In the morning, Miss Khupting would have body ache all over her body as a consequence of heave. So, their intimacy in the physical sense was not complete at that stage.

During Mr. Ngambom's stay in *thikhol khul* (abode of dead people) his parents were worried in search of him and weeping after him. So, Sangah (wildcat) intervened in this situation again and sent Mr. Ngambom back to earth. Upon reaching home, his parents' happiness knew no bounds and Mr. Ngambom disclosed to his parents what was pre-cautioned by his sweetheart Miss Khupting. Miss Khupting cautioned Mr. Ngambom that if he ever wanted to live, he should perform sacrificial rite on Lailen (river bird) and instantaneously if he ever wanted to die, he should perform sacrificial rite on Vohpi (pig). His father sarcastically repudiated to perform sacrificial rite on Lailen (bird), instead his father performed sacrificial rite on Vopi (pig), and due to which Mr. Ngambom died on that particular day as it was a taboo to do so. After his death, his spirit, too, went to *Thilkhol khul* and met Miss Khupting second time so as to stay rest of his life.[4] (Another oral tradition also says that his death was predetermined by his sweetheart by throwing down a broken piece of pot from the sky)

The love story of Mr. Ngambom and Miss Khupting depicts the depth of human love that is beyond human comprehension. The two different worlds had no panacea to control their unfathomable love. Their love had no barriers between the two worlds. Indeed their profound love transcended all physical and spiritual barriers to the extent of meeting each other again in *thikhol khul* and settled life as married couple that was incapacitated by Miss Khupting's parents. If read the story carefully, one cannot be left unnoticed the profound love prevailed between the two youngsters; their genuine love, sacrifice, devotion and commitment to have one life partner in life was amazing and beyond human words. The commitment that

---

[4] T.S. Agou Singson, *Guollui Sanakhang* (Churachandpur: Singson Printing Press,1997), 1-37.

either of them should have no other life partner in life other then they themselves is depicted strongly in the duo young lovers. This kind of love can remain perfect model for the youths of the present days against the culture of sensual love, emotional love and marriages on contract basis that are rampant in the western countries. Love in today's culture is mostly based on occasional, temporary so-called time past love, beauty driven etc.

It is also clear that their gorgeous and amazing love that was supposed to be gloriously celebrated ended catastrophically due to the parents' erroneous decision and stubbornness. Extreme stubbornness can lead anyone to take extreme step in life. Parents should have no complete control over their children's love affairs at the extreme; there must be limit, after all there is only one life to live and that must be lived to the fullest.

Their genuine love stands against the world of market and consumerist cultures in which the value of human beings is based on the haves and the haves not's. The value of a person at present trend is not based on how kind and good, caring and intelligent but is based on how much he/she consumes, accumulates wealth and money. This has become the trend of the present market culture. Market culture and capitalistic cultures alike stand for product based value that stands against humanity and compassionate heart. 'True Love Waits' is one of the most proclaimed mottos of many churches today among the youths. What Christian churches proclaim today about 'True Love Waits' was indeed fulfilled by Mr. Ngambom and Miss Khupting. Their love was so pure and divine in its characters that they accomplished their long cherished married life in their spiritual world of life after death.

5.3. Theology of Cultures in Dialogue

Song gives immense effort to doing theology with Asian resources of folktales, history as people's movement, Asian religions and, symbols and images as against traditional theology. These resources have long been devalued and demeaned as having no theological relevance in the face of dominant theology of the West and to its subsequent inheritors due to long years of indoctrination. Hence, a few considerations are taken as to bring out Song's theology of cultures and the tribal cultures as a whole and Kuki culture in particular into dialogue.

5.3.1. Tribal Spirituality and Worldview

Song identifies how institutionalized religions fail to understand each other's spirituality. Therefore he says, "The spirituality which has been developed in each religion in its pursuits of the heart of being has thus come to a quite a *sui generis* nature. Communication between one's spirituality and another becomes almost impossible feat. One's spirituality, instead of embracing other spirituality, repels it."[5] The tribal spirituality has largely been neglected in the advent of Christianity of western worldview considering tribal worldview and culture as inferior, primitive, irrational and incapable containing any good thing. Thus, Song is right that every religion has its own ways and systems to penetrate the thick veil of darkness into the heart of Being.[6] The tribals have their own way perceiving spirituality, the Supreme Being and the mysterious things. Omen,[7] dream,[8] *genna*[9] and taboo[10] as mediums through which God communicates His purpose, intention, warning, desires and wishes to the indigenous people. These help the indigenous people to live in accordance

[5] Choan-Seng Song, "Love of God-and-Man in Action: Doing Theology with Asian Spirituality," in *Doing Theology Today*, edited by Choan-Seng Song with an Introduction by Lukas Vischer (Mysore; Christian Literature Society, 1976), 42.

[6] Choan-Seng Song, "Love of God-and-Man in Action...," 42.

[7] Omen is an erring presage of God's intention and warning and it is endowed with symbolic meaning for every movement and action for the people. If omen is interpreted as the revelation from God and be sensitive to it then it enables the people to walk in the rhythm of God's directions in the midst of chaos.

[8] Every dream may not be genuine but there are unusual dreams through which God's will is revealed. People take quite seriously

[9] The word *genna* is derived from the Angami Naga word *kenna*, which means 'forbidden.' *Genna* is considered as religious practices which demands sanctity in all matters of life by observing and abstaining from daily activities and from public which is closely related with the observance of Sabbath.

[10] Taboo is a sacred interdict that takes into account the power that surrounds certain objects and activities. They were not merely matters of prohibition; they were also practices in which the directives of the supernatural were also involved.

with the will of God.[11] Hemkholun Doungel states that the Kuki Christians must know that God's revelation of His will to human beings is not only through the Covenantal Laws but also through natural laws and the human-made customary laws for those who are not abided in Covenantal Laws.[12] Thus, the customary laws of the Kuki can be considered a partial revelation of God's divine Law that guides the Kuki of the past and the present in the path of true Christian moral and ethics. Song say, "We are what we are, not what we-are-not. We are not non-apes, but human beings. Our Buddhist and Hindu friends are Buddhists and Hindus, not non-Christians. They do not find their identity in relation to Christians; they find it within their heritage because of their faith, on their own."[13] The same applies with the tribals where they do not find their spiritual heritage in the western metaphysical concept or in the context of science and reason that is insensible to them nor to the ancient Israel's context of a legalistic God (O.T), a God who is portrayed as high-voltage God ready to devour whoever goes against Him, instead of caring and loving Father.

5.3.2. Tribal Spirituality and Traditional Theology

Western theology is anthropocentric which upholds Christology as the center of theology that is committed solely to salvation of human's soul. The anthropocentric theology is 'time and history' oriented. This is in contrast with the Asian 'space' oriented theology. This new paradigm takes creation very seriously.[14] Similarly, Song says the story of creation is in a true sense the story of salvation loaded with cosmic and historical implications. Citing St. Paul's words, "The whole creation has been groaning in travail together until now" (Rom. 8:22). Creation is God's response to this cosmic

---

[11] Sashikaba Kechutzar, "Rethinking Naga Religious Traditions: An Exploration of Tribal Christian Spirituality," in *Theologizing Tribal Heritage*...180.

[12] Personal interview with Rev. Hemkholun Doungel, Associate Professor in O.T., Trulock Theological Seminary, on (2nd May 2011), age 46, Haijang village, Imphal Manipur.

[13] Choan-Seng Song, *The Compassionate God,* 64.

[14] Huang Po Ho, "A Paradigm Shift in Theology: A Holistic Redemption to God's Creation," in *JTCA: The Journal of Theologies in Asia,* Vol. 11 (2012): 77-79.

groaning. Creation and redemption are in reality, two sides of the same coin. Where there is creation there is redemption.[15] In addition to this, Heup Young Kim advocates 'Theanthropocosmic vision'[16] to be adopted as the foundation of Christian theology which confirms the true humanity can be realized only through the right relationship with God and the earth.[17] This has been Asian way of looking at creation, earth/space intuitively in which many myths and folktales profoundly vindicate cordial and integral relations of the Supreme Being, the Mystery, creations, and human beings. Therefore, on the basis of Asian and tribal spirituality and worldviews the perspective of Christian theology can be widened. Wati Longchar has encapsulated some few points of God-human-creation relationship that can be briefly highlighted below so that it can be of great resources for Christian theology.

a) A space-oriented theology conceives God as the one who is organically related to the whole of creation. This has ruled out God as monarch. Since God is an integral part of creation, God suffers pain when creation suffers, because the tribals conceive God as one who comes out from the soil.
b) A space-oriented theology leads us to understand Christ in a new way. Christ is conceived as active in every creation and not only in the hearts of the believers because Christ as the incarnate one is organically related to the total eco-system. Jesus shares His Being with the whole created order and all parts of creations are reconciled to Christ.
c) A space-oriented theology helps us to understand the work of the Holy Spirit in a wider perspective. The Holy Spirit is conceived as working in all creation not only in the hearts of the believers.

---

[15] C.S. Song, *Third Eye Theology*, 39-40.

[16] It refers to triadic communion of God, the cosmos, and humans.

[17] Heup Young Kim, "Life, Ecology, and Theo-Tao: Towards a Theology of Theanthropocosmic Tao," in *JTCA: The Journal of Theologies in Asia,* 127.

d) A space-centered theology challenges us to understand salvation can be fully achieved only in relation to the rest of the creations.

e) A space-centered theology helps us to widen our perception of history because creation becomes the basic component of the interpretation of history. One cannot interpret history without space, land and creations. It demands the human history to be studied within the context of the totality of creation as history and creation are related.

f) A space-centered theology tells us we are integral part of the earth's community. Therefore, living in harmony within the organic whole becomes the basis for authentic human existence. Hence, it helps us to see we are integral part of macro-organism.

g) A space-centered theology helps us to affirm the whole earth is God's body and thereby, the earth's resources as ecological sacrament where we have to eat and drink the blood and the body of our Lord reverently and not greedily and selfishly.

h) A space-centered theology enables us to conceive the church as an integral part of the Supreme Being and the earth. The church stands as the micro-cosmos, the church's mission cannot be confined only to human world alone. We are part of God's cosmic mission to liberate the whole of God's *oikos*.[18]

Although Song does not address the issue of land exploitation, commercialization and destruction of land in the context of technological development which resulted to displacement of the tribal culture, the people, and the ecological crisis yet his emphasis on creation or nature is integral to cultures that has been an eye opener for the theological community without which redemption is meaningless insofar Asian context is concerned.

---

[18] A. Wati Longchar, *An Emerging Tribal* , 89-92.

5.3.3. Communitarian Value System

Song observes that Asian people have been victimized by the Western industrialization and modernization. The imported value system of technological and economic developments of the West with its colonialism, have replaced the original value system of Asia. Thus, create identity crises.[19] It is very true to the tribals as a whole and the Kukis in particular where the value system of *Lom* as a Kuki youth organization, *Som/Sawm* and *Zawlbuk*, or *Morung*, as tribal institutions of training centers of self-discipline, arts, culture etc. and on the other *tomngaina/tlawmngaihna* or *sobaliba* as tribal philosophical foundations of the tribals are overlooked and to a great extent are declining in the face of modernization and globalization. Loss of mutual respect, tolerance and cultural norms are indicative of such declinations, which are resulting to cultural crisis and disturbance of eco-system. Consequently, the cultural and religious crises that have brought disintegration among the people are now beyond restoration. C. Rajagopalachari has rightly observed in this matter that "Self-restraint in expression is one of the main forms of culture. Self-restraint in conduct is a sign and an essential part of what is called culture. But self-restraint in thought is at the root of both!"[20] Thus, it is culture that controls human lives more rigidly than state control over society, of course, not undermining religious aspect. This disruption in social ethical value system of the tribals especially, in the Kuki culture which eventually leads to disintegration of the people.

The above charts are empirically carried out to indicate and figure out the status of the Kuki Christianity as to how far cultural value systems which are deemed as binding forces are declining to its own grave. **Chart No. 4** shows that there is disunity; 90% of people agreed that there was more unity among the Kuki before Christianity. The latter **Chart No. 5** displays 80% of people admitted religious aspect to be the prime cause for disunity. H. Chongloi remarks that Christianity came to the Kuki people through the back door, and

[19] James Wu, "Song (,)Choan.Seng.," people.bu.edu/wwildman/bce/song.htm – Cached

[20] C. C. Rajgopalachari, *Our Culture*, 5th Edition (Bombay Bharatiya Vidya Bhavan, 1981), 2.

its beginning was virtually abortive.[21] His statement is based on the conviction of deciphering the mystery and spiritual meaning, the entire event of incarnation, passion, dead and resurrection of Jesus Christ in the institution of *Indoi*, more clearly than through the instrumentality of alien concepts.[22] Addition to this, Letkholal Hangsing reflects similar thought over the issue of disunity that religion is the main cause for disunity. Moreover, he further reflects, "Christianity as a religion is not to be blamed but the ideology of our theologians giving birth to a new group/association."[23] This is a point to be questioned: "Could not a divided Christianity presented by western missionaries be held responsible?" Definitely it is! As a matter of fact, a religion divided brought cultural displacement and decline of communitarian value system and disunity are the consequences. Therefore, active interaction between the biblical and cultural stories of the people is the pressing need of hour so that neither of the stories is viewed stranger to one another, nor deemed as something of the past dramatization but complimenting and reciprocating juxtapositionally.

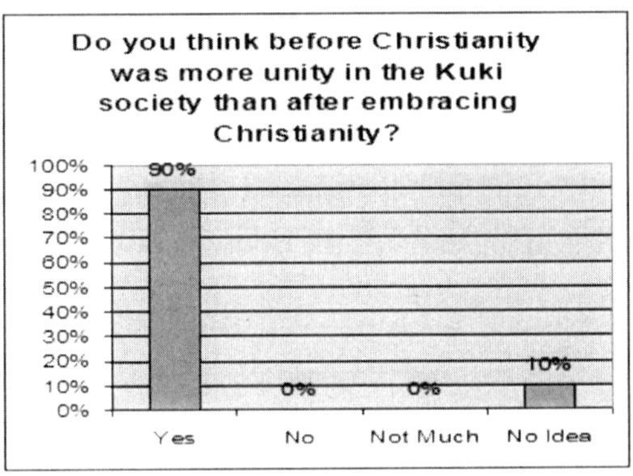

Chart No. 4

[21] Hemkhochon Chongloi, *Indoi,* 286.

[22] Hemkhochon Chongloi, *Indoi,* 286.

[23] A personal interview with Pu Letkholal Hangsing, S.D.A.O. ward-9, Medziphema town (Feb. 6th 2012), age 49, he is a M.Sc. Agri.

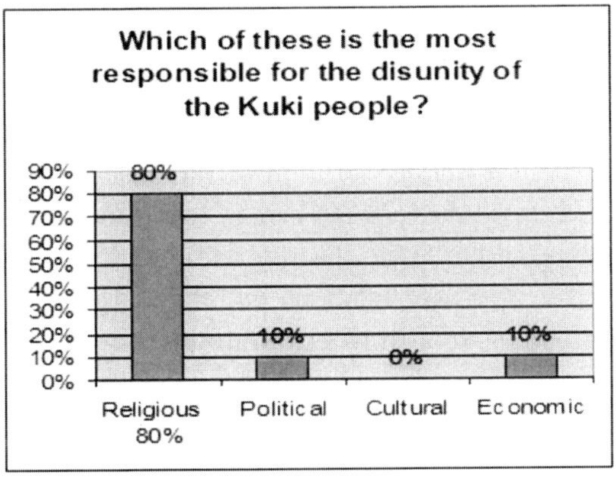

Chart No. 5

5.3.4. Religious Symbols and Images

Song opines that human beings are makers of symbols and images that give expression to who we are, how we are related to one another, to the world, to nature, and of course, to God and these symbols and images are at their most explicit in religious faith.[24] For Song, in symbols and images the dichotomy of the sacred and profane, the religious and the secular, is abolished. Penetrating them at their deepest source will make us realize that there is no question of what is Christian and not Christian. Thus, Song says, "Through exploration of symbols and images, from religious ones that have held a religious community together to the ones that serve to bring about revolutionary change in society, we may encounter a theological world in which God and humanity are engaged in struggle for human liberation both here and now and in the future to come."[25] In similar vein, the Kuki primal religious symbol of *Indoi*[26] as such

[24] Choan Seng (C.S.), "Christian Theology…," 29.

[25] Choan Seng (C.S.), "Christian Theology…," 29.

[26] H. Chongloi explicates, "*Indoi* is a bundle of several articles taken from parts of animals and plants, each of them separately imbued with sacred characteristics, bound together by a single cord made from *khaopi* (a cord made from fibre tree) plant, hung on the front porch of every Kuki house, through which the presence of the Supreme Being *Pathen* in every household is concretized."

was felt the presence of the Supreme Being in every household of the Kuki in the primal religious practice.[27] *Indoi* symbolism is the heart of all religious symbolism.[28] The Kuki worshipped not *Indoi* but God through his creation, *Indoi*.[29] *Indoi* symbolism has Christological significance; the incarnation of God in the personhood of Jesus of Nazareth has entered the realm of history living and experiencing the lot of humanity, and in doing so sanctified the profane time with his divine presence. Moreover, incarnation along with the cross-event has been testified by the Christian Church all through its history and resurrection as the assurance to humankind of the everlasting presence of God here on earth. *Pathen* who was conceptualized in the primal Kuki religious world as the Creator, Sustainer of all in the universe is now concretized in the institution of *Indoi*. Every Kuki household remains now in close proximity to the sacred. It symbolizes the manifestation, revelation and accessibility of the sacred. Thus, *Indoi* proclaims the Emmanuel of *dues otiosus Pathen,* the remoteness of God is overcome by hanging *Indoi* at the porch of the house.[30] Thus, Song has rightly said that in symbols and images the dichotomy of the sacred and profane, the religious and the secular, is abolished. It is through symbols and images a theological world encounter in which God and humanity are engaged in struggle for human liberation both here and now and in the future to come."[31] Thus, it is through institution of *Indoi* symbolism that the Kuki people encountered the Supreme Being by concretizing the conceptual *Pathen* and the dichotomy of sacred and profane is overcome. Symbols and images help us to understand the religious worldview of the people where God and humanity are engaged in our struggle for human liberation and fuller humanity.

---

[27] Hemkhochon Chongloi, *Indoi*...5.

[28] Satkhokai Chongloi, "The Unseen Christ...," 148.

[29] Satkhokai Chongloi, "The Unseen Christ...," 152.

[30] Hemkhochon Chongloi, *Indoi,* 285-286.

[31] Choan Seng (C.S.), "Christian Theology...," 29.

5.3.5. *Khankho* and Gospel

Culture as understood by Song is "not an abstract concept; it is a concrete thing. It denotes the totality of life, from social intercourse to how one conducts oneself and does business to rites of passage to religious festivals, to customs, even to legal concepts and practices."[32] In other words, "Life is culture, and culture is life."[33] The preceding discussion on *khankho* has given a clear picture of what it means to be in the context of *Tucha-Sungao-Becha-Nulam* and *Upa-naopa* relationships. As said earlier, *khankho* is acting according to what is required of one at various moments in life-to act as *tucha* (bride receiver), *sunggao* (bride provider family line), *becha* (chief manager of a family or spokesperson of one's family) as *nupa* (immediate in-laws) etc. in the social ambience of the community.[34] The second set is the *upa-naopa* reciprocal relationships; all the families are clustered into clans and have their own one Upa (in this case, head of the family) each to whom all *Naopas* (younger brothers/heads of family, subordinate to *Upa*) give the portion of meat taken from the back of an animal called *Sating*. Again *Upa* has his own *Upa* to whom he also gives Sating. Ultimately, *Sating* is given to the *Bulpipa*[35] who is the head of the Kuki people.[36] This act of life-relationships acting out in the community is quite enriching and relevant for the Kukis to be called "Life is culture," because culture as affirmed by Song is not an empty, not a concept but a concrete and denotes totality of life. Needless to say, 'theologization of *khankho*' can also be taken as another aspect. It may not be too early an idea to equate the headship of *Bulpipa* over all the Kuki clans with the headship of Christ over all Church, thereby, Christ as *Bulpipa* because Song stands against Christian faith and theology to be *sui-generis*, normative for cultures

[32] Choan-Seng Song, "From Indigenous Stories...," 109.

[33] Choan-Seng Song, "From Indigenous Stories...," 109.

[34] Hemkhochon Chongloi, "Khankhology...," 94.

[35] *Bulpi*-by virtue of being the eldest in primordial time Doungel is *upa* of all sub-clans, therefore referred to as *bulpi* of these conglomerate clans.

[36] Satkhokai Chongloi, "The Unseen Christ...," 140.

and religions outside Christianity.[37] Rather, his advocacy is to be 'relational' that is the key of doing theology with stories and reconstructing theological education in Asia.[38] Thus, speaking from relational point of view, any discrepancy may be circumvented as to rhetorically conceptualize Christ as the *Bulpipa* of the Kuki people. Since gospel incarnates in cultures, therefore, incarnation is to be understood in terms of 'historical Christ' not only 'historical Jesus.' The Word has taken human form not only in Judeo-Christian culture but also in Asian cultures,[39] and also in Kuki culture. Every Kuki individual knows it well what it means to be *Bulpipa* in terms of its deepness and far-reaching significance that hardly needs explanation.

5.4. Liberative and Negative Elements of Kuki Culture

On the basis of Song's theology of cultures, some liberative and negative points of Kuki cultural practices are worth hammering out.

5.4.1. Liberative Elements

1. Theological semantics as dealt by Song becomes very important in this respect of relationship. There is a mutual horizontal and hierarchical relationship in the practice of *khankho*. First, there is *a tucha-sunggao-becha-nulam* relationship which is enacted in mutual reciprocation. Second, there is *Upa-naopa* relationships, which are hierarchical in nature but enacted in mutual respect. When this complexity of relationship enacted out accordingly, joy, peace and love prevail in the community that is fulfilment of biblical mandate.
2. The communitarian value system in the form of *Lom, Som/ Sawm,* or *Zawlbuk* or *Morung* are of highly disciplined culture for which the youths of today can still continue to adopt with the same spirit, the spirit of sincerity, respect, self-control and spirit of dignified life that characterizes desirable biblical images. These communitarian value systems have the potentials to shield

[37] C. S. Song, "Doing Theologies with Stories Theological Education, Where Do We Go," 16.

[38] C. S. Song, "Doing Theologies with Stories..."17.

[39] Ya-Tang Chuang, "Gospel and Cultures..." 9.

and defend the youths from undesired cultures of the West such as capitalism, individualism, consumerism etc.

3. Clear understanding of religious symbolism found in the institution of *Indoi* can have better understanding about the concept of God, better access to the Supreme Being whereby the people feel God at home or feel closer. Hence, the concept of *Dues absconditus* may be overcome.
4. Song's story theology aims at interpenetrating the spirituality of the Asians, which traditional Christian churches failed it. Likewise, the tribal spirituality, that was also liberative, was neglected by the churches. It is the spirituality about how they relate to the earth/land, perceive all realities, perceive divine wisdom through myth, folktale, taboo, *genna*, dreams, omen, etc. can still play vital role in the Christian churches. One cannot deny the fact that God communicated His people through different signs, symbols or dreams. These elements cannot, at any rate, be merely reduced to unscientific, uncivilized or unchristian practice. The Bible is packed with dreams and symbols, even the end day will be known through signs and symbols.

5.4.2. Negative Aspect

1. The superfluous authority of the chieftainship of the Kuki village time to time disturbs the life of the people. Sometimes the power of the chief is over exercised which give rather apprehensive feelings to the villagers. Hence, loss of confidence that leads to severe consequences.[40]
2. Under the Kuki patriarchal system, women do not have right to access land or own a land. There is inequality of share; women are still traditionally and culturally considered inferior beings.
3. Despite the issue of women being a much-talk in the society, yet women do not come under the decision making body. For instance, there is still no women member in the village council or in the Kuki *Inpi* apex body although women have separate

---

[40] Personal interview with Dr. S. Hangsing, MBBS (Cal.), Medziphema town, Ward-9 on (6th Feb. 2012), age 61, Dist. Dimapur; Nagaland.

Women's Association that may exist as an adjunct body to the Apex body.

4. Despite the liberative elements found in the communitarian value system like *Zawlbuk* of Mizo and *Morung* of Naga, have their own limitation because they exclude women. On the other hand, *Som* of the Kuki did not constitute a proper house for their gathering in spite of its inclusivity.
5. Despite the social ethical practice of *tucha-sunggao-becha-nulam* relationship, which is well organized and revolved around the system of *khankho* yet it also has its own limitation when practically carried out. The *becha* and *tuchas* get upset usually if failed to give proper information by the head of the family.[41]

5.5. Critical Evaluation of Theology of Cultures

It is an attempt to critically evaluate cultural practices theologically with a view to draw meaningful interactions with the gospel message. To many, culture has been assumed as contrary to the proclaiming gospel since its inception of Christianity, especially among the tribals, if not the concept that culture has nothing to do with the gospel. The underlying insinuation is that there is a rift between gospel and culture, and this gap needs to be filled with sincere and creative efforts. A closer study of the case, one would certainly realize that it is rather lack of or absence of interpreting the gospel through one's cultural thought form. It is somewhat seemingly like a believer is living a dual life, gospel and cultural life without compromising each other while ironically, a believer as a cultured being is professing a religious faith in Christ. So, the dichotomy of gospel and culture is yet to overcome. There is an inseparable relation between religion and culture; it is so aptly tied with each other that one finds it difficult to draw a thin line.

Wati Longchar has expressed that even in the realm of religion and culture, the tribal religion and culture are looked down upon. Anything that does not conform to the western worldview is "devilish," "irrational," "inhuman," "inferior," "backward,"

---

[41] Personal interview with Jenny Singsit, (March 14, 2012), age 31, Sirhima Village, Dist. Dimapur, Nagaland.

"primitive," and so forth.[42] Thus, no interaction was found between gospel and culture.

On the contrary, Somen Das identifies the danger of marriage of religion and culture as equally fatal to either, since religion is so tied to the social order that it loses its spiritual character and the free development of culture is restricted by the bonds of religious tradition until the social organism becomes rigid and lifeless as a mummy.[43] This is being witnessed in our country where cultural force with religion continues to be a tradition-bound and caste-ridden culture. Thus, he further asserts that "We remain prisoners of the past and victims of socialization and internalization of our religio-cultural norms, customs and inhibitions."[44] However, the tribal Kukis and for rest of the other tribals of the North East India, cultures should not be misunderstood with the Indian culture of Brahmanism, which is hierarchically oppressive in structure. It is also worth noting that within the milieu of Kuki cultural context the impact of western cultures of diverse forms is not without non-existence but addressing such cultures are not intended here. In case, if the religio-cultural practices of the Kukis seem to have contained any oppressive element then it is rightful thing to appreciate the words of Somen Das that "Christianity is a prophetic religion of Biblical realism but not in an exclusive and absolute way. It is this prophetic element that will save a particular religion becoming identified completely with a particular culture."[45] In similar vein, what Song speaks in 'culture of empowerment' and 'culture of protest' needs to be identified. "Jesus' reign of God is not a moral exhortation; it is an indictment against society. It is not a wise counsel for political reform; it is a strong protest against the politics of the naked power. It is not a spiritual advice for change in a religion; it turns upside down the

---

[42] Wati Longchar, *The Traditional Tribal Worldview and the Modernity* (Jorhat: Eastern Theological College,1995), 9.

[43] Somen Das, *Dharma of the Twenty-First Century: Theological-Ethical Paradigm Shift* (Calcutta: Punthi Pustak, 1996), 211.

[44] Somen Das, *Dharma of the Twenty-First*, 210.

[45] Somen Das, *Dharma of the Twenty-First*, 210.

time-honoured traditions of faith and practice."[46] Of course, this may be best applicable in a situation where there is oppression and suppression yet it is not to be related to a cultural context where there is cultural-biblical productive interaction.

Again, the attempt to understand Christ from cultural thought form is not by way of indigenization because indigenization of the gospel implies the wrong notions that the gospel is something foreign but God should always be understood as indigenous to any given situation. Hence, Arvind P. Nirmal rightly observes, "the task of any indigenous theology is not to seek to indigenize a god who is foreign, but rather to seek to understand God who is indigenous to any given situation and is savingly active in the dynamics of a given history."[47] In Song's theology of cultures, or story theology the methodological presupposition behind 'indiginization,' 'acculturation,' 'inculturation,' and even 'contextualization,' is questionable. Implicit in this approach is the transforming model—the gospel transforming cultures, thus, overlooking the good in other cultures and psychological barriers still prevail.[48] In our attempt to understand gospel from the Kuki cultural context may not be that of transforming model like contextualization, nor indigenization but it is story theology that goes beyond every methodology.[49] It is by way of penetrating with a keen heart and humble spirit, into the stories especially folk stories that is familiar to most people in order to meet the Spirit of God that moves in his/ her own culture.[50] It is to understand God and gospel message in a given situation, a God is who is already indigenous and God of stories—story Maker.

Devaluation of cultural importance also gives birth to spiritual superficiality. In the words of Lalsawma, "There is an imbalance presentation of the greatest Christian word, "salvation." Instead of

---

[46] C.S. Song, *Jesus and the Reign*, 97.

[47] Arvind P. Nirmal, "Theological Implications of the Term 'Indigenous,'" in *Dialogue in Community: Essays in Honour of S. J. Samartha* edited by C.D. Jathanna (Mangalore: The Karnatala Theological Research Institute, 1982), 171.

[48] Ya-Tang Chuang, "Practicing Contextual Theology…," 148.

[49] Ya-Tang Chuang, "Practicing Contextual Theology…," 148.

[50] Ya-Tang Chuang, "Practicing Contextual Theology…," 149.

preaching the salvation of humanity, we find that Mizo Christianity preaches the salvation of the spiritual part of a person. But salvation in its fullest sense is salvation of humanity: it includes homes, culture, politics, and the economy. It also means that it is social and not individualistic.[51] So, is the same situation with the Kuki community when the church's teaching is more inclined towards salvation orientation that disorders the whole gamut of tribal socio-political-religious and cultural system. L. Seilen also underscores "... the values of primal religion and cultures are not realized and that Christianity remains an outward or foreign religion to many. The gospel seems fruitless, preaching in the churches are not properly understood, more importantly Christ remains as dramatic character like in poetries and myths. Therefore, the incarnation of Christ seems to be unfulfilled among the Kukis."[52] This may be the case with other tribes, too, as K. Thanzauva laments, "It is an unfortunate thing that many people particularly the Mizos basically understand salvation only in terms of eschatological salvation for life after death."[53] Even the mental concept of salvation needs to be liberated. He further identifies salvation with the Greek term "*soteria*"[54] meaning salvation of human beings from all that would ruin his/her life both physical and spiritual life and in the life to come.[55] Thus, this is the pressing need at this hour to re-look at gospel through the lens of past and present cultural values so that gospel of Christ which was unheard

---

[51] Lalsawma, "The Shaking Foundation of the Mizo Society," in *Reading in Mizo Christianity Series 1: Ground Works for Tribal Theology in the Mizo Context,* edited by Rosiamliana Tochhawng, K. Lalrinmawia, & L.H. Rawsea (Delhi: ISPCK, 2007), 66.

[52] L. Seilen, "The Need and Importance of Doing Tribal Theology from the Kuki Perspective," in *An Emerging Tribal Theology from the Kuki Perspective*, edited by L. Seilen (Manipur: Trulock Theological Seminary, 2011), 31-32.

[53] K. Thanzauva, "Meaning and Task of Theology," in *Towards a Tribal Theology: The Mizo Perspective* edited by K. Thanzauva (Mizo Theological Conference, 1989), 23.

[54] Matt. 9:2; Lk. 8:36; Matt. 8:25; 14:30; Acts 2:40; Matt. 18;11; Lk. 19:10 etc.

[55] K. Thanzauva, "Meaning and Task...," 23.

yet already in practice, is being carried out for better interaction with the gospel in the vertical and horizontal aspects.

The discussion on Kuki culture in light of Song's theology of cultures gives us so clear an idea that the reclaiming of cultural values is the pressing need. However, having critically looked at Song's theology of cultures, it also puts us in theological dilemma and apprehension especially if viewed from traditional stand point of view, his mission of 'enfleshment' does not accord Christianizing or converting the world but to make contribution to the renewal of civilizations deeply rooted in other religions.[56] As a matter of fact, he stands for Christ-centered mission over the church-centered mission.[57] Christ-centered mission defines the nature and function of the church and therefore, the church is an event rather than an organization, fellowship rather than church order.[58] Song has once again reminded us of the cradle of the church with the apostles when they themselves did not know the form and structure of the church because the Lord Jesus did not give any detailed rule of faith and practice except two simple rites—water baptism and communion. The forms and structure of the church grew out of the pressing needs of the time; church officers were added to meet arising emergencies (Acts 6:1-5). Initially, it actually was an event and fellowship of the homogenous belief rather than organizational and church order. There is no doubt that there are two facets of the church, visible and invisible—*visible* in the offices, in the administration of the Word and the sacraments, and *invisible* as an organism, a communion of believers. However, in the course of history as more needs aroused in the church it began to be more structural and formal, especially when the church went through the Greco-Roman world, church became more institutionalized, thus legal religion. To this fact every Christian and others alike witness the historical truth of the Christendom especially, when Martin Luther came up and protested the practice of indulgences and several others that were unbiblical.

---

[56] Choan-Seng Song, *Christian Mission,* 57.

[57] Choan-Seng Song, *Christian Mission,* 61.

[58] Choan-Seng Song, *Christian Mission,* 63.

Song has rightly observed that church is not necessarily an organizational structure or a building consisting of affiliated members with all its hard and fast rules, formalized and legalized. He reminds us of the possible vulnerability of church-mission centered over Christ-mission centered lest we merely fall prey to the grip of fanaticism and radicalism. He challenges us with his Christ-mission centered that transcends the church from its parochial confinement.

If looked further, Jesus least bothered about the ornamented and time-honoured Jewish temple of his time. Rather his ministerial fields mostly were in vales, mountains and seashores. His appearances in the Jerusalem temple were rare except on special occasions. He identified mostly with the people of low profile who in the real sense were churches, penetrating the hearts of the people through his words and deeds—these characters are indicative of church being an event and fellowship rather than mere organization. Ironically, Jesus was resorted to point out every fault of the organizational teachers of the time. Song is quite aware of the risks involved in the institutionalized churches so he prefers to use church as an event and fellowship rather than a church with order—that is organizational.

5.6. Conclusion

As has been discussed that due to cultural displacement, the Kuki ways of worship in the churches are of purely western pattern, even the message, theology, Eucharist and others are of western in character. Gospel message mixed with western culture downgrades the culture of a particular race, as such traditional songs, folktales, folksongs, dances and festivals were replaced with hymns/songs in the western tunes and dances and festivals of the West. The irony what could be felt in the church if gospel songs sung in our own and original folk tunes is that, the young and old alike would certainly feel sarcastic and unchristian. Indisputably, it is due to the long association of the churches in the western garbs. A Christianity presented to us was a Europeanized Christianity. Divisions and disunity that were rarely known in the Kuki traditional society and religion has invaded the society by way of branding different Christian denominations. This has generated fruits of hatred, contempt, disrespect and division in the community beyond restoration.

The coming of the Western Christianity with its culture of diverse forms has largely distorted the social-religious-political and cultural fabric of the people. Thus, the onslaught of the western culture of materialism, consumerism and cyber-culture has largely devastated the Kuki culture and the tribals alike. The imposition of western culture, metaphysical concept of gospel cannot fully take its profound roots in the lives of the people. Thus, detachment of one's culture bequeaths susceptibility to western culture and subsequently expose to the cultures of greed, individualism and loss of communitarian values, social ethics and spirituality are obvious.

Disintegration of the Kuki culture of human-nature relationship also leads to ecological crisis. Our analysis of *khankho* – way of life, and *indoi* – revelation of the ever abiding presence of God, which shows consonance with the gospel messages, can have viability to draw spiritual insights for renewal of the church and society. Also the analysis of communitarian value system, ethical principles and tribal spirituality, if assimilated into the church, can be enriching nucleuses of the gospel proclaimed by Jesus Christ and have larger impact upon the people.

Conclusion

The study of Song's theology of cultures from the Kuki cultural perspective in the Northeast India is resourceful and challenging in many aspects. It challenges us to re-look and re-affirm the value systems of a particular community which have for long been suppressed and deprived since the emergence of Christianity with its western garb. The study of Song's theology of cultures enlightens and assures us that culture is not opposed to gospel. Rather, gospel part takes the nature of cultures, the incarnate Christ is indicative of this. Humans are cultural beings; humans cannot be conceived without the existence of culture and culture cannot be conceived in empty space. Rather, culture is filled by the human-persons in the community. Song, based on Latin American Liberation theology that adopts Marxist critique on religion and capitalism, has identified and addressed the people of Asia being victimized by a history of western imperialism, both colonially and culturally, which creates an identity crisis for Asian Christians. Hence, Song's theology of cultures is identified with the Jesus of history than Christ of faith—the human Jesus walked through the cultural history of the world.

The present eschatological hope of the Kuki Christianity is found very strong, which may have least bothered on socio-political and cultural implication of the gospel. At this juncture Song's theology of cultures becomes very crucial. He challenges us to re-look the present from the trend of theology of incarnation afresh. The present understanding of incarnation, held by the churches, is within the frame work of past-future scheme, thus, depriving the present. Thus, this leads to the rejection of Jesus Christ as the Lord of here and now. He challenges us that the theology of incarnation should be anchored in the present as the perspective that should give meaning to the past and holding up hope for the future. Therefore, it is to assure the immediate presence of the Eternal One in the midst of temporal and transient. Hence, it is a crucial point for the Kuki Christians to understand the meaning of Christ's incarnation from the perspective of the present for its socio-political and cultural implication.

Song has opened a theological world for the tribals in particular and Asia as a whole to appreciate and critique our mentors, those Western theologians and missionaries who imposed their stereotyped theology and missiological pronouncements on our culture, religion and history, which are genetically incapable of understanding our culture, religion and history. Therefore, whatever was tribal, it was considered invalid, irrational, backward, superstitious, etc. Thus, Song's theology of cultures at this juncture becomes very important to reaffirm and re-evaluate tribal cultures in the light of their stories, myths, folktales, histories, religions, symbols and images as to grasp and identify the salvific work of God outside western Christianity.

Song has also challenged us to denounce any claim of absoluteness in any religion, for any claim of absoluteness leads to committing logical fallacy and factual error. This has ceased us to be compared with others and failed us to see the work of God in others. It is a rejection of all other claims to absoluteness. Any claim of absolute religion is inevitably a militant that tries to subject other religions or suppress them. Therefore, Song's theology of transposition from absolute to relational becomes very vital for tribals to explore their own cultural values and belief systems so that tribal spirituality is not denounced.

In a context like Asia with its multi-facet dimensions, in which every religion, community, race and tribe has its own stories of faith experiences and religious history, scriptures, etc. has something to tell to others, too. Therefore, it is quite absurd to consider Christian culture as a norm by which all cultures have to be evaluated. Thus, Song's theology of cultures becomes very significant and relevant to penetrate into Asian world taking into consideration the cultures of different peoples and nations without demeaning and devaluing any of a particular culture. At this point Song takes a staunch standpoint that every culture is equally significant and theologically redemptive, there is neither superior nor inferior culture, or normative or non-normative by which other cultures are to be judged over others, the fact that God is active in every culture.

Song's theology of cultures as an eye opener to the tribals, challenges us to retain the communitarian value systems; earth-centered spirituality, non-mechanical and dualistic view of life, religious system based on earth, the spirits of sincerity, discipline, respect, *tomngaina/tlawmngaihna*, dignified life, holistic development which are of the core teachings drawn from the institution of *Lom, Zawlbuk* or *Morung and Som* which are of the forerunners of the Christian church. These are of not something foreign or unfound in the biblical principles rather the tribal communitarian values and principles are incarnated in Jesus' gospel but going through the Western zone, it took new forms and colours so that when it was presented to the tribals mixed with foreign element and philosophized terms and jargons they are confused and not realized that those were already practiced in their former religions and cultures. So, what has sensed us at this juncture is, there was loss of connectivity between the former and latter. In addition, the social ethical vision of *khankho* which is condensed in the saying 'igol paipeh a ihetle eima paipeh a akihenge' meaning "if you first fill your friends' basket yours is also eventually filled." So is the same principle applied with Jesus' teaching, "You shall love your neighbours as yourself?"[1] This is one instance where the unseen Christ was experienced and so was the tribal Kuki *khankho* was founded in consonance with the gospel proclaimed by Christ.

Song's theology of cultures has drawn our attention what Asian spirituality means to be amidst multi-religious faith traditions where people of other faiths have their own way of perceiving

[1] Matthew 22:39; Mark 12:31: Luke 10:27.

divine guidance and vision about the path of life and salvation. Theologically, it is unacceptable to mean Christianity a normative, unique, guardian of human's salvation when others have similar vision, revelation and divine love. It is at this point that Song's Asian spirituality plays a vital role, it is nothing but penetrating into the profound heart of their religious traditions. So is with the tribal spirituality where divine wisdom, guidance, protection etc. are drawn from various phenomena such as *omen*, *genna*, taboo, dreams, customary laws, nature, land/space through which they connect with the Supreme Being. It is through these tribal spirituality that the people experience the reign of God in a more realistic ways in the sense of the incarnational terms, a perspective of the present, not of something past nor future but God's grace, help, warning, are encountered at the present.

However ironically, what is found in the research is that Christian denominationalism is one of the main reasons that causes division and disunity among the Kuki people today. Division and disunity which was unheard of or hardly heard within the Kuki community in their primal religious practice are now the most divided among other tribal communities. Under the primal religious worship of *Indoi* the people were united. Thus, the research findings may be summarized in sub-points as concluding remarks.

1. Song's story theology helps us as Kukis, tribals and Asians to inter-penetrate and inter-cultural dialogue each other into a wider community by listening to the story of success, failure, joy and pain. It helps us to affirm our theological home which is the culture and history of which we are a part by birth and association. Tribal theology in Asia which has been a homeless theology, wanderings in alien homes are coming to an end. Hence, we reaffirm our cultural theology.
2. It helps us to challenge traditionalism of faith and practices of the church inherited from the West which fail to respond and to be attuned with the oppressed and victims of the structure in any given situation.
3. Song's story helps us in opening a theological space where all stories from other parts of the world also come into play. Thus, a

theological feast of stories takes place. The story of Jesus, stories from tribals, Asia, stories in Hebrew Scripture, and stories from the rest of the world, told as stories of God's Reign.

4. Song's theology of transposition also helps the tribals to transpose ourselves from the garb of western theology to our own cultural context where a direct interplay between the biblical stories and the cultural stories take place. Hence, avoid any intervention from outside.
5. Story theology helps us to overcome the Western's compartmentalization of life which was unheard in the tribal culture. This compartmentalization of work and life dissects the tribal people in their daily life whereby confusion in the tribal society is brought in. Most common people cannot relate their lives with religious aspect, nor can't most religious leaders relate their lives with socio-political and cultural aspects.
6. Song's theology of cultures helps us to understand that the people themselves are the culture, and culture as a whole is none other than the manifestation of God's creative power translated into actual forms and events in that the "human" dimension of culture is interrelated with the "divine" dimension because culture here implies is "human beings" and not "human-made." In this case, religion as a synthesis of culture will help the tribals to affirm their cultures which were culturally-spiritual oriented.

Based on the study of C. S. Song's theology of cultures, the Kuki Christians can learn better about their culture and respect their own cultural values, spirituality and social ethical principles which are in consonance with the gospel and be quite conscious of the western cultural fascism assimilated into the Kuki culture. This consciousness of culture between their own and western can help them to overcome from cultural inferiority-superiority complex and cultural dislocation. However, the research has been not done comprehensively to its fullest and it is left open for further research for theological implication. There is much to expand and expound the rich cultural heritages based on the present finding for the future:

a. A theological study on myth, folktale etc. which is understood as story theology can be further developed for the Kuki people for enriching their spirituality where they inextricably connect with myth, folktale, land, creation, human and animals, also has immense implication for eco-theology.

b. A theological study on *khankho* which is reflected in their family relationship of *tucha-sunggao-becha-nulam* and *upa-naopa* relationship can be further studied and developed to enhance the Kuki community.

c. The study on communitarian value system of *Lom, Som/Zawlbuk* can be further studied and developed for enriching the Kuki Christian community to incorporate the other side of life other than spiritual aspect alone. It has immense capacity to revitalize the Christian community holistically.

d. One should be quite aware of the risk involved while co-relating and interpreting the gospel message in one particular context. When the gospel message is rooting itself within the culture, one should be heedful of allowing the gospel itself to prophetically interpret, challenge and change that culture and be fully understood by the believers.